The Anthropology of Contemporary Issues

A SERIES EDITED BY
ROGER SANJEK

A full list of titles in the series appears at the end of this book.

City of Green Benches

GROWING OLD IN A NEW DOWNTOWN

Maria D. Vesperi

PHOTOGRAPHS BY RICARDO FERRO

Cornell University Press

Ithaca and London

First published 1985 by Cornell University Press.
First printing, Cornell Paperbacks, 1998.

International Standard Book Number 0-8014-9322-6 (pbk.: alk. paper)
Library of Congress Catalog Card Number 84-27408
Printed in the United States of America
Librarians: Library of Congress cataloging information
appears on the last pages of the book.

Cornell University Press strives to use environmentally responsible suppliers and materials to the fullest extent possible in the publishing of its books. Such materials include vegetable-based, low-VOC inks and acid-free papers that are recycled, totally chlorine-free, or partly composed of nonwood fibers.

Paperback printing   10   9   8   7   6   5   4   3   2   1

To Arthur and Mary

Contents

Illustrations

Illustrations

[10]

About the Title
of This Book

Until recently, St. Petersburg, Florida, served society at large as a symbol of "retirement"—not only from work, but indeed from life itself. "I shudder to think of retirement," an aging Chicago pianist told Studs Terkel in an interview concerned with the meaning of work. "The most frightening thing to me will be the day I say, 'I'm going down to St. Petersburg and buy myself a little home'" (1975:338). No American reader needs to be told what this means: St. Petersburg. A green bench on the sidewalk. The end.

The fact is, there haven't been any green benches in St. Petersburg since 1961, when the city's Jaycees removed some and repainted others—any color *but* green. Among their reasons was embarrassment over a recent decision by Swift's Premium not to place an ad in the local paper because the Chicago-based meat-packing firm believed that St. Petersburg readers were too old to chew bacon (Bothwell 1975). In fact, the majority of bench-sitters in the relatively affluent 1950s and 1960s were neither frail nor poor. They were, however, old.

More than twenty years later, the green bench issue remains fresh in the minds of downtown St. Petersburg's oldest residents. "Sure they want to get rid of the old people," an elderly man told the St. Petersburg City Council in early 1984. "They

showed that years ago when they took away the green benches"
(*St. Petersburg Times*, March 30, 1984). To the elderly the
benches symbolized welcome, friendliness, and, most of all,
acceptance. They realize, perhaps more fully than anyone else,
that the city is changing. The sleepy urban center that once
welcomed them into an "ethnographic present" filled with
1920s-style residential hotels has become eager to make way
for office buildings, boutiques, and an elusive but much-antici-
pated influx of young urban professionals.

When I first came to St. Petersburg in 1975, my intention
was to study how our culture's view of old age is communicated
to the low-income elderly and how the individual older person
attempts to modify, adapt to, or reject this social construction.
I didn't realize at the time how inextricably bound together the
elderly population and its host city had become, or how deep
were the contradictions between each older person's self-
image and the image of old age held by the wider community.

I would also have been quite surprised if someone had told
me that I would eventually make St. Petersburg my home and
that I would continue my involvement with the community,
first as a member of the University of South Florida faculty and
most recently as a staff writer for the *St. Petersburg Times*. The
subtitle of this book comes from my first project for the *Times*,
a series of articles I wrote as a member of an investigative team
sent out to probe the effects of downtown revitalization on the
low-income elderly. For the first time, I was called upon to
"make sense" of aging to an audience that was not composed of
my academic colleagues, an audience that did not speak my
language. "Don't start at the end!" an editor told me. "Come to
the point, *then* worry about making your argument. People
don't want to plow through all that stuff to find out what you
have to say." Aspects of that series and observations from subsequent articles I have written are incorporated in this book.

Over the years I have become both more and less than an anthropological observer. As a writer who comes into daily con-

tact with an older readership, I have benefited from (and sometimes agonized over) the "corrective vision" that older people bring to the social scientist's perceptions of them. I have learned that the awe inspired by an anthropological researcher and the respect accorded a college professor can mask a variety of significant attitudes and behaviors among informants. My experiences as a journalist have lent new urgency to my belief that the traditional methodological and theoretical foundations of gerontology do not include an accurate understanding of what older people want us to tell them, if indeed they want to hear from us at all.

Recent surveys of aging tend to support the view that retirees, for the most part, are content with their lot. In "The Marginality and Salience of Being Old: When Is Age Relevant?" Russell A. Ward argues that "marginality appears to have little effect on the everyday lives and feelings of old people." At the same time, he admits, "Certain situations and experiences . . . may combine to make 'being old' salient, and under such circumstances the disadvantaged position of older people relative to the social structure and its values may come to affect well-being" (1984:231). Ward wisely cautions gerontologists against the temptation to define old age as a "problem." I would argue that the problem lies not with old age itself but with the way aging is perceived by the wider community.

Many of the problems of St. Petersburg's oldest, poorest residents are socially constructed—and therefore, in principle, avoidable. They stem in a strikingly direct way from our culture's view of the elderly as estranged from the future and even the ongoing present. Not only must old people meet with and respond to this distorted image of themselves informally, day in and day out, but they must contend with very material consequences, since society's formal institutional arrangements for the elderly are animated in conception and administration by that construction. In this book I tell the story of the elderly in one locality, but I also explore questions with applicability na-

[13]

tion-wide: How do old people themselves respond to the cultural construction of old age? Why do so many gerontologists, public officials, and social workers tacitly subscribe to that construction? Further, how does it inform the development and operation of public programs for the elderly?

Most Florida elderly are not poor and dependent on social services. The people I shall describe here reside in a particular section of a unique city; they are the "old old," not the "young old." Taken together, they are much like the "old old" in other Florida resort towns but unlike more recent waves of retirees, who, according to many studies, tend to exhibit more successful patterns of social and economic adaptation. Yet while my informants are perhaps a minority, they provide a most pointed example of how cultural stereotypes about aging are generated and transmitted to *all* older Americans, regardless of their socio-economic status or how they respond to quantitative surveys of life satisfaction. To dismiss the source of their problems as unique to a particular low-income subgroup would be like saying that because middle-class blacks have achieved economic parity with whites, they are no longer troubled by racism. One need look no further than the case of a young black Texas engineer who was mistakenly convicted of robbing a fast-food restaurant, or that of a middle-class black businessman who was clubbed to death by Miami police, to understand that cultural stereotypes sometimes work against even those whose external measures of well-being are high. The wealthy retiree in his beachfront condominium is shielded, to some extent, from the tangible anxieties of the low-income elderly. Yet he remains an outsider, no more welcome in the world of the young and middle-aged than the pensioner who spends his days in a crumbling residential hotel. Should he venture from the golf course to a sidewalk bench—assuming he can find one—he must grapple with the fact that to the world at large he is, first and foremost, just another "old" man.

To my informants, whose real names have not been used in this book, I owe my deepest thanks. Through them I feel that I have lived the great joys and great sorrows of several lifetimes. I thank my daughter, Corinna Calagione, who nine years ago brought to this project the enthusiasm and curiosity of a child, and today brings to it the sensitivity of a young woman. I am also grateful to Paschal Collins for his insights and assistance in the preparation of this text.

My thanks also go to various sources of instruction, inspiration, and support, including Vincent Crapanzano, Virginia Elgin, John Calagione, Elizabeth Bundy, Gilbert and Lorraine Kushner, Andrew Barnes, Cynthia Genser, Wayne Vasey, and Peter Gallagher. I extend special thanks to Kenneth Burke, who suggested Ring Lardner's "The Golden Honeymoon" as good background reading for research in St. Petersburg and advised that I should "never fail to consider the humorous aspect."

The early research for this book was sponsored by grants from the National Institute of Mental Health, the National Science Foundation, and the Administration on Aging.

MARIA D. VESPERI

St. Petersburg, Florida

City of Green Benches

Introduction

My remembrin is gettin to be pretty short. Sometimes I walk around the house lookin for somethin and it's right in my hand the whole time. I gets embarrassed when that happens. But then I look around and there ain't nobody there but me, so I figure I got nothin to be embarrassed about.

My mother used to have a bed with a big headboard, about the size of that dresser. The footboard was high, too. Mama had to have her nap, every day of her life. She used to smoke a pipe. One day she went to walkin round and round the bed, with the pipe in one hand and some t'bacco in t'other. She was mashin the t'bacco with her finger. Sister and I started to laughin, cause we knew what she was lookin for. She just kept walkin round and round the bed, mashin that t'bacco. Sister said, "Mama, what *is* the matter?"

Mama said, "It's the durndest thing, but I just can't find my pipe anywhere!"

Sister said, "What's that you're holdin in your hand?"

Then I let out a big laugh, and sister did, too. Mama said, "You can laugh now, 'cause you don't know about it yet. But someday you'll be where I am."

Selena Harper, age ninety-two

Early twentieth-century anthropologists made free use of the term "ethnographic present" to describe beliefs, rituals, and even whole communities as they existed before contact with colonial powers. The ethnographic present was a handy concept because it allowed researchers to take an apolitical stance, avoiding discussion of military and economic exploitation, forced culture change, and the impact of Christian missionaries.

As a student, I found it difficult to accept the proposition that many of the cultural systems I studied were extinct even before they were written about. Some authors found it simpler not to dwell on the fact that the pre-contact communities they described in such glowing terms were only idealized historical reconstructions. Such caveats, if they appeared at all, were often tucked into prefaces or vague references to obscure administrative documents. There was little room in the literature for informants as they often existed—disenfranchised, dispossessed, discredited in their own eyes.

If the ethnographic present existed at all, we might say that it lived in the memories of those few old men and women who had managed to hold out against acculturation. The information they had experienced it, and perhaps as they had reinterpreted they had experienced it and perhaps as they had reinterpreted it in light of subsequent change. Thus anthropologists have often, if unwittingly, presented societies as seen through the eyes of the aged. It was only with the recognition of culture change as a dynamic aspect of ethnography, however, that researchers could begin to investigate the perspective of the older person as historically and experientially distinct from that of younger generations—and that the anthropology of aging could acquire the status of a distinct subdiscipline.

The study of aging may be unique in that while, for the most part, our subjects are not ourselves, they are indeed our "selves" as we will become. Serious students of old age cannot avoid the realization that they are separated from their informants not by language and belief, but by the successful internalization of a *shared* belief system.

What confronts the anthropologist who attempts the self-reflexive task of setting aside his or her assumptions about what makes the aged "different"? The answer, for me at least, is terror. This terror springs not from a heightened awareness of my own mortality but from the realization that at some point I will be called upon to discard the identity I have developed over a lifetime and confront a social self that is essentially different, essentially old. There is no "return home" for anthropologists who study their own aged, no resumption of the comforting distances that help us rationalize our place in informants' lives.

I believe the unwillingness to confront this terror has contributed mightily to the curious sterility that characterizes much of the current anthropological literature on aging in America. With a few exceptions—Barbara Myerhoff's *Number Our Days* foremost among them—we have been loath to participate fully in the lives of our informants and to let them express, through us, the subjective nature of their encounters with the world. Instead we have adopted the methods of more orthodox gerontologists, charting and quantifying the observable behaviors of older people in the hope that we can add a little something to the broader corpus of ethnological data.

Less than ten years ago, George C. Maddox and James Wiley wrote, "Systematic development and application of theory are activities which, for the most part, have been and continue to be strikingly absent in the social scientific study of aging" (1976:17). Since that time the attention focused on aging by social scientists has increased dramatically, reflecting, no doubt, the worldwide realization that the elderly are the most rapidly growing segment of the population.[1] Yet, while gerontology has attracted the quantitative methods of the sociologist and the clinical methods of the psychologist throughout its rel-

1. At the United Nations World Assembly on Aging held in Vienna in 1982, UN demographers released the following projection: "People aged 60 and over continued to be the fastest growing population group in the world and will number 1.1 billion in 2025." Put another way: "In 1950, the 60-plus group's size equalled a little more than the population of the Soviet Union; by 2000 it will equal more than the projected population of Europe or of the projected sum for the United States and the Soviet Union; by 2025 it will be nearly equal to the projected population of the western hemisphere." (Oriol 1982:17.)

atively brief history as an interdisciplinary social science, it has only recently adopted the participant-observation methods of the anthropologist. Relative late-comers to the field of aging, anthropologists have been left a bit perplexed as to how they might best model their inquiries. If Maddox and Wiley's assertion that gerontological research has not been systematically grounded in theory remains valid, what informs the increasing body of information provided by social scientists in both academic and applied contexts? What has prevented existing theoretical constructs drawn from several fields from being successfully applied to the phenomenon of aging?

For the most part, researchers have seized upon social role as the point of departure in studies of later life. Jennie Keith points out that "old people in industrial societies are . . . stranded in the liminal. Exit signs are clearly marked, but reincorporation is not on the map. Their choice is between cultural bushwhacking and clinging to the crumbling cliff of midlife roles" (1983:207). Although many researchers have described how role loss occurs in Western cultures, few have asked why it does—perhaps because the answers seem so firmly linked to the process of industrialization.

Childhood, another victim of industrial change, has been the subject of much cultural introspection. We are not content to say that children are dependent, alienated, or uprooted simply because they are children. We want to know how children experience their lives—how it feels to be regarded and treated as a child amid a variety of conflicting social messages. "Old age," however, remains an unexamined cultural construct. We may ask what it is like to *be* old, but rarely how it feels to be *regarded as* old. Of course, *le regard de l'autre* has always been central to the concerns of social psychology, phenomenology, and existential philosophy. The issue of interior versus exterior views of reality has also fascinated anthropologists. Not content simply to record what people do, we seek to learn why they do it and how they feel in the process. The immediate problem, of course, is that our observations and interpretations are, of necessity, shaped by our own cultural categories. This issue is important in both the realm of methodology and the writing of ethnographic accounts.

The need to transcend established methods of investigation and analysis was first dramatized for me in 1976, when I attended the twenty-fifth annual Southern Conference on Gerontology in Gainesville, Florida. In addition to the traditional academic debates, this conference provided a forum for discussion among state officials and applied workers in the field of aging. Among the principal speakers was seventy-seven-year-old Max Friedson, president of the Miami-based Congress of Senior Citizens. An articulate, angry, and often abrasive speaker, he generated an atmosphere of perceptible discomfiture among the researchers and theoreticians who attended his lecture.

Friedson spoke about reality, but not the simple, life testimony reality of an old person describing how it feels to be old. He focused instead on what older people see when they regard themselves in the mirrors set up by social scientists:

> This is the first time . . . that we have been invited to let us tell them, the academians, what we want rather than they tell us what we want. And I want you to know that it's a delight for me—for the first time, in all the years that I've been spending fighting for the elderly in Tallahassee and going to these various seminars. Most of the grants that are being given to the people around shouldn't be given, because it's a waste of money in most cases.
>
> Let me just tell you some of these monies that are being spent, our tax money. I was invited to a seminar in the ——— Hotel, a very fine hotel: "Sex and Senior Citizens." So I went down there; I thought maybe I'd find something new. After listening for about ten or fifteen minutes I raised my hand. I says, "Doctor, if we didn't know how, you wouldn't be here!"

Implicit in Friedson's ironic remarks was the suggestion that the priorities of gerontological research would be quite different if researchers allowed themselves—temporarily at least —to take the perspective of their informants. Instead, social scientists have traditionally sought to measure the aged from a distance, that is, against standard adult role expectation models. A formidable body of quantitative data has been amassed, charting the formal relations between individuals and their kin, peer, and employment networks. Yet researchers have often done violence to the experience of their informants by focusing on the effects of role loss rather than its cause. That the old form a discrete social category—identified by custom—is an assumption social scientists share with the rest of American society. It is my belief, however, that attention must be shifted from the category "old age" to the context of aging, and that old age itself is not a discrete social or even physical caste. The cultural construction of old age is a process; it is the concretization of abstract, unexamined assumptions within the context of everyday interaction.

Clear manifestations of this concretization emerge through language. For instance, one says of the thirty-year-old that she *has* a full life but of the eighty-year-old that she *has had* a full life. Society shifts its cultural description of the aged person to focus on the past. It is true that the past is carried forward within each individual until death; yet, like the rest of us, older people continue to experience life fully in the ongoing present as well. This contradiction between description and experience is the source of the greatest potential distortion for the social observer and the deepest alienation for older people themselves (Merleau-Ponty 1962:69-72).

In the absence of a fully developed cross-cultural perspective, we tend to view "age" and what it measures as concrete universals. Students of anthropology, for instance, are often taken aback when they first discover that people in some societies "don't know how old they are." And while Americans may eventually come to understand that our perception of the ordering, passage, and accumulation of events is rooted in Western *ethos,* there is little in everyday life, or in the social scientific literature for that matter, to reinforce a culturally relative view of age.

Gerontologists have indeed observed that it is necessary to distinguish between physiological and chronological aging, and chronological aging has rightly been identified as a cultural phenomenon.[2] Less clearly recognized, however, are the wide discrepancies between culturally agreed-upon chronological symbols and the ways individual older people may feel about themselves. In her classic literary/philosophical study, *The Coming of Age,* Simone de Beauvoir described how the awareness of aging is imposed on the individual from without—by the quickly masked expression of uncertainty which precedes recognition by a long-absent friend, or the automatic gesture of a young woman who surrenders her seat on a crowded bus to an elderly man, thus marking him not as male, but as old. "In our society the elderly person is pointed out as such by custom, by the behavior of others and by the vocabulary itself: he is required to take this reality upon himself. There is an infinite number of ways of doing so: but not one of them will allow me myself to coincide with the reality that I assume. Old age is something beyond my life, outside it—something of which I cannot have any full inward experience" (1972:291).

The pervasive frustration experienced by gerontologists who attempt to apply existing theoretical models to the study of aging is caused by a failure to examine the underlying cultural constructs that contribute to both our initial conceptualization of the category "old age" and our subsequent attempts to analyze this phenomenon in its own terms. The most basic of these constructs, and the one that must bear closest examination, is our cultural construction of *time*.

2. C. Davis Hendricks and Jon Hendricks provide an excellent overview of this topic in "Concepts of Time and Temporal Construction among the Aged, with Implications for Research" (1976:13–49). See also Husserl (1964) and Minkowski (1970).

Introduction

In American society, time is conceptualized as continuous, linear, and cumulative. Each individual is made aware of the development of self through reference to cultural chronology. From childhood, he or she learns to assess personal progress in any domain with reference to an abstract, temporal dimension. The concept of time provides a number of significant symbols for the child. It is perceived as an objective unit of measurement, useful in the differentiation of days and weeks, the ordering of events, and the relative situation of self with respect to the "ages" of others.

Throughout life, we attempt to maintain a close relationship between cultural chronology and our conceptualization of human physiological, psychological, and social development. Our description of the human life span in ongoing, linear terms implies a potential for infinite development. As Sartre (1963:96) noted with regard to Western culture: "Society is presented to each man as a perspective of the future and . . . this future penetrates to the heart of each one as a real motivation for his behavior" (see also Schutz 1971).

Yet while the calendrical accumulation of time seems infinite, the individual's life span is predictably and observably limited. Once physical maturity has been achieved, we shift emphasis to other areas; the notion of growth is extended beyond the physical to include emotional and intellectual development brought about through the accumulation of experience over time. Among the young and middle-aged, for instance, a "mature" person is one whose emotional development is judged to equal or exceed that expected at his or her chronological age.

Yet, as a person ages, physiology reasserts itself, and contradictions between the theoretically infinite potential for personal "growth" and the demonstrable finitude of every human life span become apparent. Eventually, society ceases to perceive the individual in abstract, temporal terms, and begins instead to regard him or her as representative of an all-too-

[26]

concrete process of physiological disintegration. This change in conceptualization from without is accompanied by a change in cultural classification; at this point the person is no longer regarded as middle-aged or mature but as old.

In no instance, however, is there a concomitant shift in orientation for the individual. The older person is not provided with a conceptual means to reconcile his or her sudden negation by a future-oriented terminology with previous expectations about the nature of experience in the ongoing present and in the future.

What does occur is an increasing sense of confusion about the application of temporal symbols to the description of self. Since society does not mediate its substitution of a finite temporality for an infinite one, the person can no longer decode what his or her age "means" to others. Thus a cluster of significant symbols, specifically those referring to temporal orientation, encode unmediated contradictions that become increasingly problematic for the individual in old age (see Bateson 1972:244-78).

To return again to the question of language, consider the grammatically parallel sentences "He's a success at twenty-five" and "He's a success at eighty-five." I have experimented often with these sentences by asking a succession of students to interpret their meaning. The first statement seems clear; all students have agreed that the crediting of success at age twenty-five implies unqualified cultural approval. The second sentence is ambiguous, however. Some students have opted for the interpretation, "He's *still* a success at eighty-five—you know, sort of like George Burns or somebody." They have suggested further that this sentence is parallel to the first—although for different reasons—since *continued* success at eighty-five is just as remarkable as initial success at twenty-five. Other students, however, read the sentence to mean: "It has taken him eighty-five years to become successful." In other words, the aged subject is damned by faint praise.

[27]

I would argue that such dilemmas of meaning confront older people in their everyday interactions, forcing them to explain themselves through reference to the past in an attempt to compensate for culturally constructed interpretations of "age." Unfortunately, this ontological dilemma is also reflected in the structuring of our analytic systems. The contradictions inherent in our socio-temporal situation of the individual survive in the theoretical models we construct to explain social process.

In a powerful, well-documented, and enduring book, Robert Butler (1975) identified a variety of stereotypes that he referred to as "myths" about aging: "the myth of unproductivity," "the myth of inflexibility," "the myth of 'senility,'" "the myth of serenity." Here the word myth is taken according to its most prevalent contemporary meaning, as a fixed idea or constellation of ideas which is erroneous, uninformed, or prejudiced. An anthropological definition of the word provides a slightly different perspective: "Myths display the structured, predominantly culture-specific, and shared, semantic systems which enable the members of a culture area to understand each other and to cope with the unknown. More strictly, *myths are stylistically definable discourses that express the strong components* of semantic systems" (Maranda 1972:12–13; italics in original).

This focus upon the "components of semantic systems" provides the foundation for a theoretical model that takes into account the underlying cultural assumptions that contribute to our identification of old age as a concrete category. The identification emerges through rhetorical manipulation of semantic components, both at the level of everyday interaction and at the level of social scientific analysis. Such a perspective allows one to consider the delicate interplay among the aging individual, the culturally significant symbols that constitute the medium for his/her discourse with others in society, and the rearrangement of this interaction—as narrative—by the social analyst. As de Beauvoir so eloquently described, the aging individual experiences an eventual breakdown in the "ability to take the attitude of the group to which he belongs" (Mead

[28]

1956:33; see also Berger and Kellner 1970). It is evident that this breakdown is closely linked to contradictions in our perception of the human life span as inherently limited and yet subject to a nonfinite, socio-temporal system of measurement. The gerontologist may be aware that widowhood, retirement, poverty, and institutionalization represent aspects of this disrupted discourse which are socially or circumstantially generated and imposed on the individual from without. Yet the very analytic narrative that the gerontologist constructs to explain the ontological status of the old—the ordering and sequence of events against which theoretical models are drawn—is itself circumscribed by a culture-bound conceptualization of the life process.

It is not surprising that the majority of older Americans rarely identify with what we have written about them or with the policies we have formulated to ensure that they remain within the social fold. In the words of a rather indignant Max Friedson: "One grant that was issued was for babysitting. We originated that, and we do it for free. Still, they have to teach us, train us, how to babysit. It seems ridiculous, to think that people of our age who have raised a family, raised the children, and we've got *great-grandchildren* . . . along comes a young person who just got Bar Mitzvahed and they tell us how to babysit!"

The writing of this book fell naturally into two parts, in line with the ongoing development of my observations about St. Petersburg's low-income elderly. Part One is concerned with the symbolic processes whereby older people apprehend and subsequently accept, reject, or renegotiate a variety of messages about aging received from an urban community in transition. Part Two explores the question of whether the goals of specific social programs aimed at low-income retirees reflect more accurately the needs of those who are served or the perceptions of those who serve them.

PART ONE

The Apperception
of Old Age

Who is it that is giving us the feeling that we are alien? The greatest danger that we face is believing any of the garbage that society is trying to lay on us.

Ched Smiley, age seventy

[1]

City of Green Benches

People who declare that there are no activities for old age are speaking beside the point. It is like saying that the pilot has nothing to do with sailing a ship because he leaves others to climb the masts and run along the gangways and work the pumps, while he himself sits quietly in the stern holding the rudder.

Cicero
Cato the Elder on Old Age

My family and I arrived in St. Petersburg on a humid, 90° October afternoon. Hot, hungry, and tired, we drove to the nearest motel and spent the remainder of the day in air-conditioned splendor. Our motel was located on a state highway, one of those neon strips studded with fast food restaurants, chain stores, and a topless lounge—"Showcase of Suncoast Talent." The tourist season had not yet begun, and the empty parking lots looked rather desolate. From this perspective, St. Petersburg seemed like any other semi-urbanized, commercial area in the "New South"—far too much space devoted to far too many hastily constructed, gaudily painted fast-buck enterprises. I began to wonder: What makes *this* the best-known retirement city in America?

The next day I set out to find the city government buildings, hoping to secure census tract maps and any other information that might help me discover the most suitable neighborhood for fieldwork. The character of the urban landscape began to change as I drove east toward Tampa Bay. *Here* was an old resort town, complete with Spanish-style stucco and postcard-perfect subtropical foliage. I approached a crowded little park in the center of the business district and stopped for a red light. Suddenly I received a real shock—of the thirty or more people who stepped off the curb to cross a busy intersection, almost all were old. A number of them were using canes, some had walkers, and one man in a wheelchair raced against the light to mount the opposite curb. These were the people who rarely ventured out alone in Boston or New York, my standards of measurement. I knew I had arrived.

Pinellas County, with an estimated 2,739 people per square mile in 1984, is the most densely populated county in Florida. It is also one of the fastest-growing areas in the state. During 1980-83, Pinellas gained 38,278 new residents, an average of 1,063 per month. Interestingly, however, the percentage of *older* residents has actually dropped in recent years. According to 1975 estimates, Pinellas contained the state's highest percentage of residents age sixty-five and older. More significant, Pinellas also contained the highest absolute number of residents in this age group: 224,323 out of a total population of 666,595. By 1980 the county's population was estimated at 728,531, 39.5 percent higher than in 1970; yet during the same period the percentage of elderly dropped from 29.5 to 27.8, with an absolute number of 202,825. Between 1970 and 1980, the median age fell from 48.1 to 45.8 years. Estimates for 1984 by the University of Florida Bureau of Economics and Business set the county's population at 766,809.

In 1984 the median age of St. Petersburg residents, who number 240,933, is 42.2—making it slightly "younger" than the county as a whole. The highest concentration of retirees is found in the downtown section of the city, where the median age is seventy-three and 44.9 percent of the population is over seventy-five. In this ninety-block area, bounded on one side by Tampa Bay, the median age has continued to rise while the absolute number of retirees has decreased in recent years. In other words, the center city "old old" are dying off and are not being replaced by younger retirees.

These statistics give several clues to the importance of St. Petersburg as a center for the study of aging. In St. Petersburg, as elsewhere, a recent focus on downtown revitalization has gradually eaten away at the housing, shopping, and entertainment resources that made urban living attractive to generations of retirees on fixed incomes. Yet unlike most cities, St. Petersburg once courted this very population, claiming them as the bread and butter of economic stability and inviting them to relocate—sometimes sight unseen—from communities more than a thousand miles away. In recent years, the long-established assumption that St. Petersburg is an "appropriate" place for the retiree of modest means has created a unique set of problems and responses for older residents and for the urban community as a whole. To understand the impact of social change on an elderly population that has constituted itself, in large measure, according to a now-defunct set of cultural expectations, it is necessary to explore the history of St. Petersburg's identity as "Green Bench City," or, less kindly, "Wrinkle City."

During the annual meeting of the American Medical Association in 1885, Dr. W. C. Van Bibber of Baltimore delivered the results of his research to find the ideal location for a "World Health City." The site chosen was Pinellas Point, Florida, situated on a small peninsula in the Gulf of Mexico. As often happens, this pronouncement from the medical community inspired a "movement" of sorts. By 1895 a Philadelphia promoter had attracted significant numbers of the hopeful to the "Health City," recently incorporated as the village of St. Petersburg. Many of them were wealthy—a fact that translated rapidly into a thriving downtown.

A series of land speculations and ambitious, sometimes fanciful business enterprises rose and fell over the course of the next ninety years. A real estate boom began in 1912. In 1914, the world's first commercial airline began flights across the wide bay that separates downtown St. Petersburg from Tampa. Major league ball teams took up residence in the opulent downtown hotels during spring training. Over the years, the St. Louis Browns, the Philadelphia Phillies, the Boston Braves, and the New York Yankees have walked the streets of downtown St. Petersburg. (Today the Mets and the Cardinals make St. Petersburg their winter home.) Top names in entertainment made their way to St. Petersburg during the 1930s, where they attracted huge crowds at the Coliseum Ballroom.[1]

Through it all, St. Petersburg remained a mecca for the elderly, the physically infirm, tourists, and drifters. Lacking the commercially navigable harbor and natural resources that helped Tampa develop as a center of commerce and industry just twenty-five miles away, the "Sunshine City" settled on a foundation of tourism, suburbanism, and the related service industries.

St. Petersburg is laid out on a modern grid pattern, divided by a principal thoroughfare (Central Avenue) into north and south sections. It is bounded on the east by Tampa Bay and on the west by a series of Gulf barrier islands. Early settlement was concentrated along the Bay. It is here in the old downtown that the opulent tourist and residential hotels remain, although several have been torn down or converted to other uses.

One of the area's earliest resident landowners was John Donaldson, a former slave, who settled in what is now St. Petersburg shortly after the end of the Civil War. Many of modern St. Petersburg's oldest black residents arrived during the late 1910s and early 1920s from rural Alabama, Georgia, and South Carolina. Women were attracted by the availability of service work in hotels, restaurants, and private homes. Men came for railroad or construction work and stayed on to become small-

1. For more on the early history of St. Petersburg, see Bothwell (1975), Grismer (1924), Dunn (1973), Fuller (1972), and Hurley (1977).

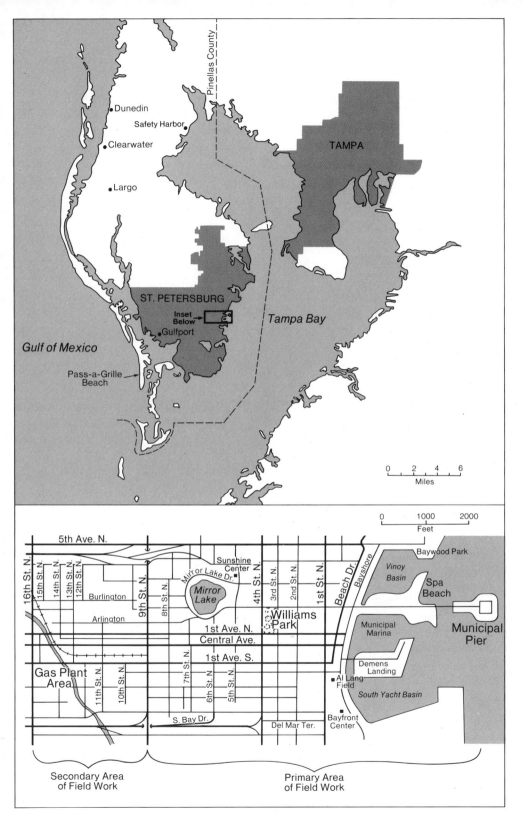

Downtown St. Petersburg

scale entrepreneurs. Residential segregation was strict: blacks were confined to several self-contained but interconnected neighborhoods known as "Methodist Town" and the "Gas Plant" section. These neighborhoods were located, literally, on the other side of a set of railroad tracks bisecting Central Avenue about a mile west of the main business district.

As St. Petersburg spread northward, southward, and westward over the years, a pattern of center city decline became apparent. Younger whites and the more well-to-do elderly built homes away from the downtown. Younger blacks moved from the vicinity of Central Avenue into the south sections of the city. A new generation of tourists was more captivated by the Gulf island beaches than by the wide verandas and formal dining rooms of Tampa Bay hotels. For more mobile younger residents, suburban malls replaced Central Avenue stores as the place to do business. Many of the large homes built by wealthy newcomers in the 1920s were divided and subdivided, spawning a low-rent district for retirees. Landlords further maximized their holdings by erecting tiny efficiency apartments over existing garages, also popular with elderly renters.

As a result, age segregation became spatial as well as social for retirees on modest pensions. Until recently, many younger people refused to visit the downtown at all unless they happened to work in banks, stores, or office buildings. "Too many old people." "Nothing to do." Conversely, many old people did not patronize the mid-county malls, which they considered too expensive or too far away.

The original downtown neighborhoods still contain the highest concentration of white retirees. Social clubs, dances, and sports activities for "seniors" are located in this area, as is the city's "multi-service senior center," built in the late 1970s. Public and denominationally sponsored high-rise housing projects for the old are also situated downtown. Cafeterias, thrift shops, and dime stores service primarily an older clientele. Since many downtown retirees do not have private transportation, their social and economic transactions are often limited to these neighborhoods.

Serious downtown revitalization efforts began in the 1970s, when St. Petersburg embarked upon the most recent in a series of urban renewal projects. Historically, these projects have earned mixed reviews from the general public; some have served to generate antagonism between the business community and older downtown residents. In 1961, for instance, the City Council voted to repaint and/or remove several thousand "green benches" from city sidewalks—benches the older residents clearly believed were put there for their comfort and enjoyment. This seemingly minor issue marked the emergence of a social and economic estrangement that has troubled St. Petersburg ever since. Consider the tone and choice of arguments in this description of the event, compiled by *St. Petersburg Times* columnist Dick Bothwell for a Bicentennial publication called *Sunrise 200:*

> It has been estimated that there were some 3,000 benches on downtown streets. But considerably less than that were returned. Wear and tear, said the Jaycees.
>
> The old heave-ho, said furious oldsters.
>
> "How could you be so cruel," one lady wrote the movers and doers via *The Times,* "as to take away those Green Benches which have made the West Coast famous, and at the same time deny the Senior Citizens who in most cases live from day to day to meet their friends there?"
>
> Well, you might say it was because business people felt that the city's national image was going downhill fast. There were little hints. Such as Swift's putting a full-page ad in the *Tampa Tribune* rather than in *The St. Petersburg Times* because an advertising executive in Chicago thought St. Petersburg residents were too old to chew bacon!
>
> This lopsided view of the Sunshine City had been growing over the years. The business community writhed each time a national publication added to the warped image.

[39]

1. Central Avenue, 1937 (Burgert Bros., courtesy Hampton Dunn)

Said *Holiday Magazine* in 1958: "The old people sit, passengers in a motionless streetcar without destination."

Said *Life* in 1958: "Lonely and bored, old people pass the time listlessly on a St. Petersburg, Fla., sidewalk . . ."

What really tore it, though, was a 1960 report from First Research Corp. of Miami. The report said a shocking number of industrial consultants, queried in a poll, checked TRUE instead of FALSE a statement that about 50 percent of St. Petersburg's population was 65 or older. (In 1950, the percentage was 22).

The report also warned that the green bench image had gained great currency in the nation.

Hence the Ad Club's campaign commenced, heating up the old, old argument: Is a bench a symbol of leisure and friendliness—or decrepitude? (Bothwell 1975:76–77)

Another multivocal symbol, the "Million Dollar" municipal pier building on the city's waterfront, was demolished in 1967 in favor of a unique modern structure shaped like an inverted pyramid. Older people regarded the "new Pier" as another joke at their expense in the city's attempt to revamp its image; young people didn't know *what* to make of it. Shops and restaurants came and went under the disinterested gaze of the pelicans and fishermen loitering outside. By all accounts, the 1926-vintage "old Pier" was shabby and rambling but always crowded—a great social gathering place for retirees. The "new Pier," on the other hand, has never attracted consistent patronage among the young or the old.

By the mid-1970s Tampa boasted sparkling new skyscrapers, a fancy airport and an NFL team, complete with stadium. St. Petersburg, labeled "God's waiting room" in an April 20, 1970, *Time* magazine article, was determined to make some headway in the race to attract major investors. Once again, the elderly were targeted as an obstacle to urban renaissance. Eager to draw new companies to the area, a downtown redevelopment coalition known as St. Petersburg Progress commissioned the New York and Chicago–based Fantus Company to do a mar-

2. Central Avenue, 1960 (Bruce Tibbo; courtesy *St. Petersburg Times*)

3. Green bench graveyard, 1969 (Tom Bennett; courtesy *St. Petersburg Times*)

4. Central Avenue, 1984

[44]

keting feasibility study. Heading Fantus's list of recommendations was an observation about the retirement city image: "Nationally, the name St. Petersburg conjures up an image of a community which is dominated by a population 65 years of age and older." The city was advised to "re-establish St. Petersburg's image as a community consisting of young, progressive citizens" (Fantus Company 1977:49,4).

Fantus researchers based this recommendation, at least in part, on interviews they conducted with local businessmen. According to their report: "Most executives felt that St. Petersburg has to overcome the image of being a city which caters exclusively to the elderly. The stigma of the 'green bench' must be substituted with the image of a community which is vibrant and quite alive" (p. 24). Also irksome to local leaders, Fantus reported, was "the large percentage of senior citizens which appear to aimlessly walk around downtown St. Petersburg during working hours" (p.30).

I came to St. Petersburg in 1975, two years before the Fantus study was written. Informants reported that the physical landscape of the city was basically unchanged from what it had been in the 1950s, yet there was a strong undercurrent of anxiety about the future and a clearly articulated belief among the downtown elderly that they were no longer wanted. By mid-1979 the only grocery store and shopping center within walking distance of downtown had gone out of business. In 1980 my oldest informant, age ninety-eight at this writing, was evicted from the rented house where she had lived since 1916 to make a way for a proposed industrial park and baseball stadium. By 1984, local business leaders had invested millions in renovations designed to attract "young, progressive citizens" with money to spend in the newly established Central Avenue boutiques and restaurants.

I could not foresee these rapid changes when I began fieldwork among St. Petersburg's downtown elderly. My original project was a study in symbolic interaction, an attempt to un-

[45]

derstand how culturally constructed "messages" about old age
are communicated and how they shape the older person's self-
concept. My vantage point was a duplex house in a downtown
neighborhood where 73 percent of the residents were sixty-five
or older. While there were plenty of apartments for rent in this
area, moving into one wasn't so easy. In fact, my telephone
contacts with absentee landlords provided my first insights into
the cultural construction of old age in St. Petersburg: "How old
are you? You don't really want to live *there*." "You say you have
a small child? Forget it. The neighbors don't want any kids
around."

As it turned out, my daughter was quite popular in our
adopted neighborhood. Many people wondered out loud why
they didn't see more children. Her presence often facilitated
the establishment of friendships with older people, who
seemed hungry for contact with the young.

My research sample for the initial 1975-76 fieldwork year included ninety low-income older people, approximately 50 percent white and 50 percent black. Although the proportion of
blacks in this sample was not representative of the population
at large, it was only a slight oversampling of the group within
my radius as a resident of the downtown area and as a partici-
pant-observer in the activities of social service agencies serving
the low-income elderly. In addition, older blacks have been in-
strumental beyond their numbers in the historical formation
of the community and in the ongoing development of urban
St. Petersburg. About 7.6 percent of Pinellas County residents
are black; 17.2 percent of St. Petersburg residents are black.
Many of my oldest black informants were able to provide invaluable first-hand observations about what life was like in St.
Petersburg during the 1920s, 1930s, and 1940s. Most white informants, on the other hand, retired to Florida during the late
1940s and 1950s.

About thirty members of my sample became principal informants, people with whom I had repeated personal contact. I

visited with them on a regular basis, collected life history material, accompanied them on excursions or to social events, and often established contact with their relatives or close friends. I maintained more formal relationships with the other sixty, who appear in my notes as traditional case studies. Many of these were members of social clubs or clients of social service programs where I had observer status. I had only occasional personal contact with them, but ample opportunity to observe their behavior and to discuss my observations with others who knew them.

I observed interaction in a number of residential settings, including individual and single-family units, public and private housing projects for the elderly, residential hotels, and state-subsidized boarding and foster homes. I also made contact with a total of twenty-two social service agencies that offered programs for older people, including mental health agencies, outreach, congregate dining, and adult day care.

Additional material was collected from a variety of secondary informants—volunteer workers, store clerks, restaurant workers, and others who had daily contact with an older clientele. For many of the more socially isolated elderly, a waitress or "that nice lady in the thrift store" provided the primary source of social interaction. Awareness of the nature of these informal contacts was highly significant for my later assessment of the impact of redevelopment on low-income retirees. Younger neighbors were also deeply involved in the lives of informants, and their perceptions were crucial to my understanding of how stereotypes about old age are generated and transmitted through social discourse.

I have had ongoing contact with this community of elderly people and with the wider St. Petersburg community in the years since my original fieldwork was completed. In 1978 I joined the faculty of the University of South Florida in Tampa. In 1979 the *St. Petersburg Times* asked me to serve as consultant for "Growing Old in a New Downtown," a special series

[47]

detailing the effects of redevelopment on low-income retirees. The following summer I joined the project's investigative and writing team, which included Peter B. Gallagher and Ricardo Ferro of the *Times*.[2] I became a member of the *Times* staff in 1981.

Thus I have been blessed (and sometimes cursed) with the opportunity to observe how my informants respond over time to the changing messages they receive from a rapidly evolving urban milieu. I have also had many opportunities to observe how the young and the more affluent aged act on their perceptions of downtown retirees. It is here in the interstices of daily living, in the commonplaces of conversation and the "informal formalities" of social interaction, that the cultural construction of old age unfolds.

2. "Growing Old in a New Downtown" was published in eleven parts, April 26–May 6, 1981.

[2]

Reciprocity

The essential requirement of reciprocity is, that basing myself upon my own teleological dimension I should apprehend the other man's. . . . Apart from some exceptions, the
old man no longer *does* anything. He is defined by an *exis*,
not by a *praxis*: a being not a doing. Time is carrying him
towards an end—death—which is not *his* and which is not
postulated or laid down by any project. This is why he looks
to active members of the community like one of a "different
species," one in whom they do not recognize themselves.
                    Simone de Beauvoir, *The Coming of Age*

De Beauvoir, Sartre, and Minkowski are among those who
have emphasized the dialectical nature of the relationship between past and future, between future and present, and between present and past. Above all, the significance of the future is seen as the animating force in human activity. Without a
future, the individual suffers what Minkowski has identified as
"a gap between one's own life and ambient becoming, as well
as a feeling of impotence and very often of distress" (1970:311).

It is easy to see that for many older people the future seems
devoid of possibilities for positive action. The fact that such a
limitation is culturally imposed is frequently masked by the
popular assumption that older people *prefer* to live in the past,
figuratively speaking, or are perhaps literally compelled to do
so by the effects of "senility."

While conducting research among nursing home patients

(Vesperi 1975, 1983), I was struck by the fact that many residents seemed to "forget" the present, while past memories remained intact. For them, it seemed easier—and in some ways more practical—to escape into a time when they were still regarded as useful adults than to dwell on the implications of their current life situations. Among the noninstitutionalized aged, recent memory loss is quite selective in its choice of victims. It is often linked to drastic life changes such as the death of a child or spouse, relocation, or a seemingly unrelated accident or disease. It can often be decelerated or even reversed when the individual is presented with appropriate social challenges or psychological stimuli.

I do not mean to minimize the fact that a percentage of older people do suffer from true organic brain syndromes, or that the memories of others have been impaired by adverse drug interactions, congestive heart failure, malnutrition, or severe depression. What is peculiar, however, is that the behavioral symptoms associated with a cluster of diseases have come to dominate our cultural construction of how the "typical" old person should behave. It appears that the symptoms of a selective pathology are not only acknowledged but indeed *reinforced* as normal behavior.

To understand how this behavioral constellation has come to be associated with aging and how that association continues to be reciprocally reinforced by young and old, it is necessary to examine the content and context of social encounters. In each of the following cases, note the subject's use of temporal distortion in an effort to manipulate or compensate for the perceptions of others.

Emil Dawson

I met Mr. Dawson while I was accompanying an outreach worker from Neighborly Senior Services, a local agency that provides a variety of community-based programs aimed at keeping the frail elderly out of institutions. Mr. Dawson, who had been referred as a potential candidate for adult day care, lived in a small boarding home in south St. Petersburg.[1] We were met at the door by a middle-aged black woman, the owner, who made us comfortable in the well-furnished living room and then went to find Mr. Dawson. This took a while; Mr. Dawson walked very slowly with the aid of a cane. With some difficulty, he lowered his large body into a chair and assumed a polite but guarded expression.

In answer to the preliminary questions on the intake form, he explained that he was eighty-two years old and a widower, and that he was born in a small Massachusetts city. He had no children; his closest relative was a niece who lived in the North. Despite his obviously impaired mobility, the only health problems he would acknowledge were digestive troubles and the fact that he was "hard of hearing."

Mr. Dawson maintained an attitude of polite attention during the questionnaire session and subsequent description of the day care center's philosophy and goals. Interpreting his cooperative attitude as consent, the outreach worker attempted to conclude the interview by setting a date for the organization's minibus to pick him up. Mr. Dawson's hearing seemed to deteriorate suddenly; he had to be told about the bus schedule over and over and seemed to be stalling for time. Finally, the outreach worker attempted to pin him down: "How about Monday?"

"OK, Monday morning will be all right. And I'll . . . try it out and see if I like it. If I do, why . . . (brief silence). The only, the only trouble is, you see, uh . . . I don't know how to explain

1. Most boarding homes are run as reputable businesses or as "family style" living situations. Others, however, leave much to be desired. The disabled or chronically ill elderly are particularly vulnerable to substandard living conditions. Boarding home owners have occasionally been known to rent rooms "by the hour" or to encourage prostitutes to solicit elderly male residents. See Chapter 4, below.

this but, uh . . . every since I got old, I enjoy being with younger people. I don't, I dunno why it is but it's always—it's been that way. I don't, uh, I don't care about being with people my own age. For some reason or other it just pales on me; I don't like it."

"Well, how old do you consider young?" the outreach worker asked.

"Huh?"

"How OLD do you consider YOUNG?"

"Well, I'd say, uh, up around fifty, that's all right. But, uh, I don't like to travel with people . . . uh, I don't, I just don't get along . . . well, I *get along* with most anybody but I mean I, I just uh, I always have, since I got, since my wife died, in fact. She was considerably younger than I was and I always, uh, preferred younger people. At least. Because I'm eighty-two; I'll be eighty-three in July and . . ."

At this point the outreach worker changed the subject abruptly by asking Mr. Dawson a technical question about his Medicaid coverage. He then tried, once again, to conclude the interview with a perfunctory, "Are there any questions that you have?"

"Well, no, uh . . . where do you *go* as a general rule? Uh, do you go places?"

The outreach worker provided a brief description of day to day activities at the center.

"No games?" Mr. Dawson asked.

"We do have games, a lot of games. Shuffleboard, darts, things like that."

"Shuffleboard, I've never tried it. I'd like to try that. Darts I've played, but I never tried shuffleboard."

"Well, you'll see how you enjoy it then. OK?"

"I will, yeah," Mr. Dawson replied absently. "I will. Monday."

Back on firm ground, the outreach worker again attempted to clinch the deal: "Our bus will pick you up Monday morning," he said firmly. "Somewhere between 8:30 and 9:30, I'd say. OK?"

"I'll get the lady of the house to give me a little early breakfast," Mr. Dawson offered. "She generally don't feed me till 9:30. I get up around eight o'clock, myself. I'm used to getting up earlier than that but I . . . they, uh, you have to go by the house, after all. The lady feeds me good and everything and they treat me good here."

"Good," the outreach worker said wearily.

"I was up at the————(nursing home) after I come out of the hospital," Mr. Dawson continued confidentially, "and, uh, I'll tell you the honest truth—I kind of gave up on my own race. From the treatment I got from the white people up there. And, uh, 'course the aides was all colored and I don't think there was one of them up there that wasn't my friend. But the white head nurse and, uh, there was only one white registered nurse up there that was decent to me. The others, uh, for some reason or other seemed to *hate* me. And I couldn't figure it out. I'm a big man. I weigh over 200 pounds. And uh, you know what they fed me for breakfast? A small sauce dish with oatmeal or Wheatina, cream of wheat . . . a small glass of milk, a small juice, one slice of toast and a cup of coffee. Now I can't live on that, let alone get my strength back. And uh, so I went—I had the aide that was in my room, at that time I couldn't walk—I had her wheel me down in the wheelchair to the main desk. And I asked for more food. Why that head nurse and that redheaded nurse grabbed that wheelchair and they rushed me back to my room. And the head nurse says to me, 'Mr. Dawson, you're insane.'

"I says, 'I'm insane? Why am I insane?' And she spit out a long word, technical term or something or other. I said, 'Am I insane because I asked for more food?' I said, 'I'm as sane as you are.' I said, 'I'm *hungry*. I'm a big man and I want to get my strength back.'

"Most of the people in there, they just live in a wheelchair

and a bed, that's all. From the wheelchair to the bed, the bed
to the wheelchair. But I wasn't figurin on that. I was figurin on
getting my strength back and getting out of there. So, uh, you
see, when I came out of the hospital, I was sixteen days goofy
in the home up there. I had hallucinations, nightmares, strange
dreams, things like that. I told strange stories, and uh, I asked
different nurses that took care of me while I was in there if I
ever was offensive. Because I figured maybe that was the reason these white people don't like me." At this point, Mr. Dawson interrupted himself with a laugh. "'White people.' Listen
to me. As though I wasn't white myself!

"And uh, they said, 'No, Mr. Dawson, you were a perfect
gentleman as far as that went. But you had strange stories to
tell, and you, uh—those nightmares and hallucinations, things
like that.' And they told me some of 'em and they were strange,
I'll tell ya."

I interrupted Mr. Dawson at this point to ask if he was given
drugs in the nursing home. He turned to me with a sudden display of interest, although he had barely acknowledged my presence earlier in the interview session.

"I don't *know*," he continued thoughtfully. "Uh, in the *hospital* they gave me these drugs, but I can't understand it. I've
been in the hospital for a very serious operation and they only
gave me a spinal; I was awake all during the operation. But
what kind of drugs did they give me that would last for . . . I
must have been out of my head when I *left* the hospital,
and sixteen days in the [nursing] home. One night around two
o'clock in the morning I wake up and I see a hearse in my
room. And six men with an empty coffin are coming toward my
bed. Can you imagine? And I hadn't even walked but I managed to make the door and get out in the hallway. And there
was a wheelchair there and I went head over heels and skun my
knee and the nurses come out—heard the rumpus—and they
come out and I remember one of them saying, 'Oh no, not

again!' Because I was with a roommate now, you see. They said, 'What's the matter, Mr. Dawson?'

"I says, 'There's a hearse in my room.'

"They said, 'No, there's no hearse in your room; we'll show you.' A couple of 'em helped me into the room and sure enough, the room was empty.

"And Christmas Eve, I went to bed around eight o'clock and I woke up around eleven. I look out into the hallway, and I, I hear girls laughing and talking and they're decorating—to *my* mind they're decorating the hall out there for Halloween, not for Christmas! I'm saying to myself, 'What are they doing decorating for Halloween? It's Christmas!' But luckily I rolled over and went to sleep, and I woke up in the morning without any trouble or anything. I hope I don't have any more, that's all . . .'"

The outreach worker, who had heard enough, seized this pause as an opportunity to terminate the conversation. "Well, I'm sure. We'll look forward to seeing you starting Monday morning, OK?"

Mr. Dawson took the hint, but he never appeared at the adult day care center.

The Messrs. Dawson of this world seem doomed to be abandoned in mid-sentence. Others invariably find them tedious, difficult to follow, boring. At worst they are labeled "wanderers," that is, incapable of remembering the original context of a conversation. I would suggest, however, that the tendency to tune out this type of monologue is a central factor in our cultural construction of old age. Perhaps if we listen a little more closely, we can understand why Mr. Dawson and the well-meaning outreach worker failed to communicate.

It is first necessary to examine the exchange as it was constructed according to the outreach worker's expectations. His goals when interviewing a potential program participant were as follows: first, to determine whether the subject was eligible for adult day care according to the program's criteria of age and physical or social need; second, to provide the day care center staff with pertinent medical and social background about the subject; third, to acquaint the subject with the center's activities and goals so that he or she could decide whether or not to participate in the program.

Mr. Dawson's responses to parts one and two of the interview were deemed appropriate by the outreach worker. He answered most of the background questions accurately and concisely, with no deviation from the subject at hand. Had this been a test of "reality orientation" he would have passed with flying colors. At part three, however, Mr. Dawson began to "wander"; his responses became inappropriate within the context of the interview. This was most striking because he had asked very few questions during the outreach worker's description of programs and activities at the adult center. As he seemed coherent and capable of understanding what was said, the interviewer interpreted his lack of comment as implicit consent. It was at the moment when he was asked to make a commitment—"When would you like to come . . . ?"—that Mr. Dawson began groping for ways to restructure the narrative in accord with his own needs.

Many of those who have contact with older people in St. Petersburg, from doctors and social service workers to store clerks, bank tellers, and switchboard operators, express frustration when confronted with a person like Mr. Dawson. "It takes forever to fill out a simple form." "Old people never stick to the subject." "They always end up talking about themselves." Many interpret this as an indication that the older person is removed from everyday life and thus incapable of fully understanding the context of interaction. "Can't he see that I have other customers?" Others assume that the older person's attention span is so limited by the effects of "senility" that he or she will inevitably wander. "Poor old lady, she just can't help herself." What is often not recognized is the fact that while the young and middle-aged operate on the level of manifest content, the older person must seek to manipulate discussion in order to reveal the latent content, that is, what the outsider thinks of him or her.[2]

The encounter between Mr. Dawson and his interviewer provides a good illustration. The outreach worker was a well-dressed young man who spoke authoritatively and carried a clipboard full of official-looking papers. Mr. Dawson was at an immediate disadvantage; the presence of such an interviewer in his home suggested that he could be regarded as a helpless old man who was no longer capable of functioning without the intervention of a social service agency. Attempting to make the best of what he perceived as a compromising situation, Mr. Dawson attempted to dispel the interviewer's assumptions by transforming the narrative context from one of *supplication* to one of *reciprocity*. The interviewer asked questions; Mr. Dawson provided correct, concise, "helpful" answers.[3] The outreach worker signaled the end of this reciprocal exchange when he decided that Mr. Dawson should be enrolled in the program. In asking him to set a date, he was seeking Mr. Dawson's affirmation of his conclusions.

It became evident immediately that Mr. Dawson was *not* prepared to accept this interpretation of his life situation. Reluctantly and with some embarrassment at first, but later with

2. My use of Freud's interpretive term, "latent" content (1967), is intended to suggest the multilevel structure of such encounters. Here the outsider recognizes only the established social formula appropriate to the interaction. The older person, on the other hand, has already sustained repeated blows to his or her self-image and is highly sensitized to the powerful condensed expressions of age stereotyping that may emerge. He or she may become more concerned with the assessment of these symbols than with the manifest goals of the encounter.

3. This desire to establish a structure of reciprocal exchange occurred often in my contacts with informants. Once a person understood that I was a student conducting research under government sponsorship, he or she was usually eager to "help." The two most common responses to my requests for information can be paraphrased as follows: "I always like to *help young people get ahead*." or "Maybe if the government reads about me it will *help other old people with their problems*."

increasing conviction, he expressed his dislike of "old people" and his reluctance to be publicly associated with the adult center. It became clear that the presence of his late wife, as someone "younger than I was," had provided a buffer against socially enforced age segregation. As long as he was accepted by people "up around fifty," he could resist the outsider's intrusion upon his self-image.

Mr. Dawson's resistance was evident on another level as well. His lengthy discussion of the hospital and nursing home experiences can be understood not as inappropriate wandering but as well-reasoned attempts to defend his autonomy. Mr. Dawson's account of his experience in the nursing home reveals that he was fully aware of the staff's attitude and of the unspoken code of behavior and expectations: "From the wheelchair to the bed, the bed to the wheelchair."

Based on my own work with nursing home patients, I would conclude that his experiences were, unfortunately, quite typical. However, most patients are so demeaned by such treatment that they soon acquiesce to staff expectations. Mr. Dawson's level of awareness was exceptional; his attempts to preserve his self-image against assault were tangibly rewarded when he was released from the nursing home. It is significant that this monologue began directly after the interviewer's third attempt to conclude the session with a commitment from Mr. Dawson. Faced with what he perceived as a new danger —adult day care—he drew upon these "war stories" to bolster his self-confidence and to signal that he was capable of preserving his independence.

In this light, it may appear inconsistent that Mr. Dawson should choose to relate his hallucinations, as these would seem to support the outsider's view that he was not in full command of his mental faculties.[4] It was here that he deliberately shifted the narrative again to suit his own needs. Beneath his recitation

4. This type of hallucinatory experience, known as "sundowning," is a common one for older people in new settings (see Curtin 1972:135).

of nightmares and strange stories was a question: "I can't understand it . . . I can't understand why . . ." Having re-established himself as a strong, future-oriented individual—"I wasn't figurin on that. I was figurin on getting my strength back and getting out of there"—he was able to regard us once again as objective "experts," perhaps capable of providing the answer to a question that perplexed him. Indeed, he correctly interpreted my question about drugs as a signal that he should continue, despite signals to the contrary from the interviewer in charge.

Mr. Dawson felt obliged to execute a series of temporal and contextual shifts in order to remain on a reciprocal basis with the outreach worker. As Alice discovered during her first encounter with the Red Queen in *Through the Looking Glass*, it took all the running she could do just to stay in one place. In Mr. Dawson's case, the "place" was not merely a physical setting but a social one as well. To return again to de Beauvoir: "The essential requirement of reciprocity is, that basing myself upon my own teleological dimension I should apprehend the other man's." In order to bring about this apprehension in the eyes of another, the older person is often forced to construct a multidimensional, multitemporal reality. In the process, he or she may inadvertently reinforce the other's preconceptions about the experience of growing old.

Alice Dunn

I encountered Alice Dunn while I was accompanying Lydia, an outreach worker for Pinellas Opportunity Council.[5] The

5. I made many contacts and gathered a great deal of demographic information during the early stages of my fieldwork by "tagging along" with outreach workers from various social service agencies. Ideal for this purpose was a door-to-door survey conducted in 1976 by Pinellas Opportunity Council, a service and advocacy agency that operated under the auspices of the Community Services Administration (formerly the Office of Economic Opportunity).

two women had met about a year earlier, when Alice's car ran out of gas near Lydia's house. Alice happened to live in the census tract that Lydia was canvassing, and Lydia felt that she might need information about food stamps.

Alice was a tiny lady, about seventy years old, with dark brown skin and long black hair. A stroke had left her with a serious speech impairment and a weakened right hand and arm. Her small dirt yard was dominated by a large collard patch, surrounded by an improvised chicken wire fence. A splintered board carried the hand-lettered warning: BEWARE BAD DOG. Bad dog himself was chained at the far side of the yard.

Alice motioned us to come inside. We entered through a narrow kitchen and sat down in the small living room. The predominant feature here was a large color television set. Lydia wanted to fill out some welfare forms for Alice, but Alice's speech was so slurred we could not make out her answers. I suggested that she might fill out the forms herself. She got out her glasses and studied the papers, then shook her head and held out her arm to indicate that her hand was too weak to grip a pencil. Lydia questioned her about this, asking if her arm was painful and if she had received any therapy. Alice left the room briefly and returned with a bottle of wintergreen. Lydia rubbed some on Alice's arm, and also rubbed in some encouraging words about the possibility of enrolling her in a physical therapy program. Alice just smiled.

Eventually we decided to consult the man we had seen scraping paint from the front of the house. He told us that Alice was only her nickname, that she had been a school teacher during her working years, and that she "had some Indian in her." If we wanted more information, he suggested, we should wait around for Alice's husband to come home from work.

"What does he do for a living?" Lydia asked.

"He takes care of the graves," he answered, motioning in the direction of a high-walled cemetery at the corner of Alice's block. He grinned at Alice, then continued: "Every night when it's time for dinner, she just goes to the door and calls him.

Some night he just ain't going to come out!" They both laughed uproariously; it was obviously a long-standing joke.

Alice showed us a picture of herself as a young woman; it was an eerily beautiful, delicately colored portrait in a carved frame with curved glass. Encouraged by our expressions of interest, she brought out a framed photograph of a young man in military uniform, then a snapshot of the man with his wife. She pointed proudly to the pictures and then to herself—"Mine." This was followed by a carefully preserved basic training yearbook; she challenged us to pick out her son from the rows of regulation young faces. We both guessed wrong.

Later we drifted out to the collard patch. Lydia offered her a dollar for some greens but Alice shook her head violently. She made it clear that we, as her guests, were welcome to all we could pick, but that she would *not* accept any money. In the end, Lydia, Alice, and the painter did the picking; then I collected the greens in an old shopping bag.

Alice hugged and kissed us both before we left. On the way back to the agency, Lydia told me that no one "messed with" Alice when she went to the store because she always carried a gun in one hand and a knife in the other. "The cops see her," she added, "but they just let her alone."

Alice Dunn provides a more direct example of the function of reciprocity in the maintenance of dignity and equality. Like Emil Dawson, she chose to steer the discussion toward a more active phase in her life; she showed us pictures that demonstrated her maternal role and her identity as a beautiful young woman. Alice, like Emil, was also sensitive to outsiders' perceptions of her poverty and obvious disability. While she made no effort to disguise either, she refused to accept us as representatives of a welfare agency. She treated us instead as visiting neighbors and offered us food from her garden. In this way she managed to reverse the conditions of obligation while reaffirming her status as a self-sufficient individual.

Lydia's final comments provide some insight with regard to

Alice's self-concept. Alice lived in what was considered a "high risk" neighborhood for older people. To reach the nearest grocery store, she had to pass by the cemetery where her husband worked. Groups of boys congregated behind the cemetery wall where they could not be observed from the road. These boys sometimes preyed upon old ladies, stealing their money on the way to the store or their groceries on the way home. As a result, most elderly female residents of the neighborhood were afraid to pass this corner unaccompanied.

Despite low crime rates overall, older people in downtown St. Petersburg are aware that their appearance marks them as potential victims. Sadly, many respond by removing themselves from the criminal's visual field, that is, by hiding in their homes. Alice, on the other hand, decided to compensate for her appearance with a visual cue of her own. By carrying unconcealed weapons—and neighborhood lore held that she was perfectly capable of using them—she successfully avoided the potential victim label and thus maintained, through compensation, a degree of the autonomy enjoyed by younger people.

Carlotta Burke

Carlotta, age seventy-nine, was a former concert pianist from New England. She was severely crippled by arthritis and walked with two canes, yet she was determined to keep up her social contacts. Carlotta was a very attractive woman; she dressed with great care and always maintained a cheerful demeanor, even when suffering severe pain. She continued to play the piano beautifully, yet would respond to any compliments with a self-deprecating reference to the past: "I *used* to play in concert halls, but now . . ."

The following fragment of conversation was recorded during preparations for the wedding of Carlotta's friends, eighty-three-year-old Amy and Richard, age seventy-five. The wedding was held at the adult center where the couple met because Richard had no family in St. Petersburg and Amy's grown children were vehemently opposed to the marriage.

"Let me come in, I'll play the wedding march. (Hums a few bars.) It's been a long time since I even thought of such a thing. I'll try and play it by ear now, you know. I just play by ear now, can't remember it by note. Play by ear . . ." Carlotta broke off suddenly, lowering her voice. "I didn't even know Amy, she's got a wig on."

"That's not a wig; that's her hair," I explained. "She had it done."

"*No.*"

"Yeah."

"*Really?* I thought it was a wig!"

"Somebody told me her friend that's a hairdresser, as a present, had her hair done special like that." (It was dyed blond and styled.)

"My, I didn't know—I didn't *know* her! I looked at her twice before I could know hardly it was Amy. Honestly. I kinda liked the gray on Amy. I mean, you know, it looked more natural I suppose."

"For a special event," I suggested.

"But then when you get married, you got to look young and uh, spry, you know, and *chipper*," Amy stated.

"Oh, I don't know," I said noncommittally.

"It makes a difference! I'd probably do the same," she insisted.

"But you don't fool anybody but yourself," an elderly male bystander added cynically.

Amy looked a bit flustered. "Yeah. Oh boy!" she agreed hastily. "That would be the day, that I'd go to blond. Or go to dark. If I ever put myself to blond you know what they'd say? 'Mother is getting senile. She's getting nutty.' They'd think I was just 'bout crazy if I ever did a thing like that."

"What, dye your hair?" I asked.

"Oh yes, they'd think I was getting senile. They'd think something was getting into my brain, or I'd got in my second childhood, you know. That's what they'd think. Daughters and sons like their mother kind of motherly and all. And when I put on that dark wig—remember my dark wig?—it had gray in it but my son looked at me, he said, 'Just what are you trying to be,' he says, 'a sixteen-year-old? What's the matter with you?'

"Why you'd think I committed a crime 'cause I had that on. You see, I had that wig a long time, when I was younger. And then I got the *gray* one and I wore it more, you know. Then I thought why not go back to the other one? When I went back, Ron [a bus driver] liked it. He told me it made me look younger. A few people said that so I began to wear it." She laughed wistfully. "Get some good out of it!

"This is a big day for those oldsters. I hope they'll be very happy. I . . . you know . . . I just hope everything turns out real nice for them . . . I think he's the lucky one . . . Yep, he's a lucky man."

For purposes of comparison, I would also like to include the remarks offered by Frank Murphy, age seventy, part-time janitor in the building where the ceremony was held.

"Jeez, I been here since 8:30 this morning waitin for this wedding." He paused, then added, "*I* been married three times."

"Have you?" I asked politely.

"My first wife died. Second wife, twenty-eight years, couldn't make it. This one here, nine years—she started the same stuff. Running 'round, drinkin. I said, 'Nah, I ain't gonna spend twenty-eight years with you, kid. Either you go or I go.' So now, I just got my divorce, and I got my final papers a coupla weeks ago. I'm a free man now. I don't think I'll get married again. I think I'm gonna do like the younger generation does. If I meet a nice girl—shack up. Ya know what I mean?"

At the beginning of this chapter I commented on how the most negative aspects of aging have been codified into a normative model for all older people. As a defense against being judged senile ("They'd think something was getting into my brain") Carlotta chose to "grow old gracefully." For Carlotta, growing old gracefully meant examining each behavior against standards set by her children, upon whom she felt completely dependent, and by her peers, whose delight in her music provided her major outlet for reciprocal involvement.

Carlotta was painfully aware that Amy's children did not approve of the marriage. She was quick to signal her agreement with the younger generation: "It's been a long time since I even thought of such a thing." (Remember that her association was as *friend* and *contemporary* of the couple.) She then effectively thwarted any potential compliments about her musical ability: "I just play by ear now." This led immediately to a discussion of Amy's hair and the inappropriateness of trying to look younger. She remarked that gray hair looked *more natural*—except in a context where an older person has already exceeded the bounds of propriety: "But then when you get married, you got to look young and uh, spry, you know, and *chipper*." She placed particular, sarcastic emphasis on the word "chipper."

Carlotta eventually perceived that I approved not only of the marriage itself but of the bride's appearance as well. She wavered momentarily: "I'd probably do the same." Yet as soon as a member of her own age cohort voiced his disapproval, she immediately reversed herself again: "That would be the day, that I'd go to blond." Carlotta reinforced this reversal by calling upon her family as the final arbiter of appropriate behavior among the aged. She made it clear that the punishment for "ungraceful" aging was to be judged senile, nutty, or crazy. Even a small deviation such as wearing a "youthful" wig could only be justified when bolstered by frequent expressions of approval from others.

For Carlotta Burke, "growing old gracefully" meant grad-

[65]

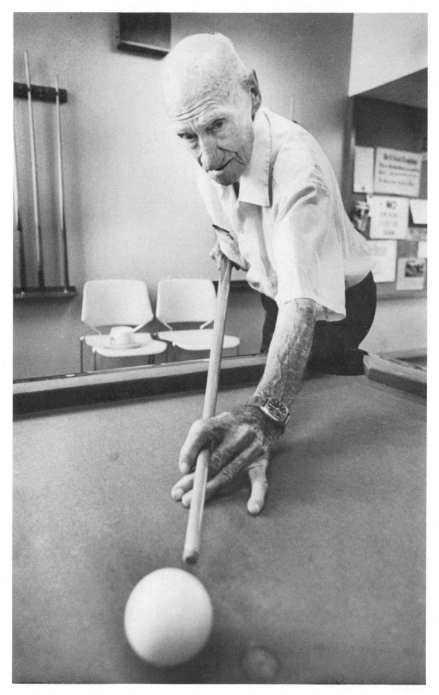

5. Game room, Sunshine Center

6. Checkers game, Sunshine Center

7. Round Lake

8. Spa beach, on Tampa Bay

ually discarding her pre-established adult identity. It was no longer appropriate to accept compliments on her musical ability, as a younger person would do. It was also no longer appropriate to attract attention to her personal appearance, as a "sixteen-year-old" might.

Keeping in mind that these associations were called up within the context of a marriage between two elderly people —perhaps the ultimate inappropriate situation in the eyes of the young—it is interesting to contrast the remarks of Frank Murphy (also a friend of the couple). Unlike Carlotta, Frank lived alone, held a job, and prided himself on his independence. For him, association with the wedding ceremony held no connotations of the inappropriate or ridiculous. Engaged in an ongoing reciprocal relationship with society, Frank could view the marriage of his contemporaries as an occasion for introspection about the past and speculation about the future. Frank drew upon his observations and experience as *resources available to him in the ongoing present* for the construction of future life projects.

As a final comment on the wedding, and one that perhaps needs no elucidation, consider these observations by Selena Harper, a ninety-two-year-old woman who had worked until age eighty-seven as a domestic. She lived alone in a high-rise apartment complex for low-income elderly.

"I think it's nice, she want a husband and can *git* one. I think it's nice for her. An I know he's glad to git her, 'cause they say she's the only one's got anything. He's glad to get hold t'it. You wouldn't blame him.

"I'd git one [a husband] if I could," she added with a laugh. "I don't blame her, 'cause she doin good as she can . . . Yeah. I used to say I wouldn't do this an I wouldn't do that. You don't know what you'd do. You don't know what you *gonna* do. You may know what you don't *want* to do, at that time, but your mind gits changed . . ."

Emil Dawson and Carlotta Burke find themselves in life situations where they are defined *a priori* as dependent and childlike. They exist as supplicants, not as partners in reciprocal exchange. The supplicant is a shadowy form, an empty coffer; he or she receives but is not expected to give in return. Thus the identity of the giver (child, service worker) as a socially engaged being is reinforced while the older person is judged impotent.

When confronted with the need to concretize identity—and even the most simple conversation demands the presence of reciprocating identities—these older people must scramble to "recreate" the self. In the process, distortion is inevitable. Emil Dawson must draw upon a variety of seemingly extraneous past experiences. Carlotta Burke must dissemble, denying the very basis for her claim to recognition as an interesting or worthwhile person. Each has been bound by socio-temporal encompassment. Unlike Frank Murphy, Alice Dunn and Selena Harper, who have retained high levels of reciprocal status in the community, they no longer feel free to be themselves.

[3]

Recognition

". . . Curious the effect our own appearance has on us in a photograph, even on a plain card, when we look at it for the first time. Why is it?"

"Perhaps," I answered, "because we feel that we are fixed there in a moment of time which no longer exists in ourselves; which will remain, and become steadily more remote."

"Perhaps," he sighed. "Always more remote for us . . ."

"No," I went on, "for the picture as well. The picture ages too, just as we gradually age. It ages, although it is fixed there forever in that moment; it ages young, if we are young, because that young man in the picture becomes older year by year with us, in us."

"I don't follow you."

"It is quite easy to understand, if you will think a little. Just listen: the time there, of the picture, does not advance, does not keep moving on, hour by hour, with us, into the future; you expect it to remain fixed at that point, but it is moving too, in the opposite direction; it recedes farther and farther into the past, that time. Consequently the picture itself is a dead thing which as time goes on recedes gradually . . . and the younger it is the older and more remote it becomes."

Luigi Pirandello, *Shoot!*

We have all experienced the sense of estrangement described by Pirandello. Our immediate response to an old picture is that of recognition—acknowledgment of one's self —often followed by a sense of detached amusement: *Yes, that's me. Imagine, I used to dress like that!* On the level of sheer resemblance, the photograph is truly "fixed in a moment of time which no longer exists in ourselves." Yet the impact of such a picture goes far beyond a comparison of mirror images, a mere chronicle of physical aging.

One afternoon at an adult day care center in St. Petersburg, participants arranged old photos of themselves on a long table. Everyone lined up to examine them. The initial discussion consisted mostly of chuckles and sighs: "I used to be so much thinner." "I looked so *funny* with my hair like that!"

This soon gave way, however, to explanations of each picture's social context. If a photograph aroused feelings of sadness and regret—and many did—it was not regret for the lost image of oneself but for the context within which that image had existed. For instance, two women displayed pictures of themselves in formal evening clothes, each accompanied by a well-dressed man. For the first, whose husband had since died, the picture served as a reminder of her isolation and sorrow. For the second, whose husband was still living, the picture gave evidence of ongoing happiness. "That's how we looked then," she said softly, "and we've been together these forty years since." Both women were less concerned with the isolated portraits of themselves as attractive young people than with their images as social beings. A picture became remote only if the particular bond of recognition it represented had been broken.

One man shared a snapshot of himself in a Boy Scout uniform, taken on the day he had marched in President Wilson's inaugural parade. The man's father, whom he mentioned often in conversation, had been a government scientist. This photo, which generated the most enthusiasm from the group, served a dual function for its subject. It reminded him, privately, of a secure and happy boyhood; on a public level, it set his childhood experiences within a familiar time frame. Everyone remembered President Wilson. Once this context had been set, other people became perceptibly more interested in the details of his childhood reminiscences. For them, one man's family memories served as the symbol of a shared era, bridging the gap between private and public experience.

Old people who remain within their natal communities can usually depend on the public memories of kin and neighbors to provide a context for their past experiences, to keep social photographs "alive." Eighty-year-old Mr. Jones, long retired, is still "the postman." Miss Smith is still "my third grade teacher, and my mother's teacher before me." To recognize is to *know again*, and as such, an act of recognition must be based on shared experience of the past.

For older people who have retired to new communities, the experience of daily living can be like showing faded photographs of themselves to a stranger. *They* continue to recognize themselves, not only as physical but as social presences. The stranger, on the other hand, sees only a picture, a "dead thing," a fixed representation of the past. Very quickly, the stranger becomes bored. Moving to St. Petersburg, relocating to a high-rise development, and becoming a participant in a social welfare program are all activities that disrupt established relationships with significant others. If the older person has nothing to show but a frayed photo of an unshared past, he or she can never hope to be recognized.

Downtown St. Petersburg's white elderly are mostly jobless, sometimes bitter, and, by today's standards, poor. For the younger people who hurry by a group of old men in the park or grip their steering wheels impatiently while a frail woman struggles across the street, it's hard to imagine that the old folks weren't always "that way." Most of them, in fact, were once solid, middle-class couples, confident that their retirement nest eggs would last a lifetime. Then came inflation, bereavement, urban renewal. It makes no difference that they once owned big homes, drove new cars, hosted holiday dinners for hordes of loving relatives "up North." To the young, who share no part of their social history, these facts are not even faded photos, they are muddy negatives.

The black elderly tend to fare better in this context, in large measure because they share an unbroken social history with children, grandchildren, and "great-grands." Within the family, the neighborhood, and the church, old age often fosters increased recognition and respect.[1] Within the wider St. Petersburg community the black elderly receive little or no recognition, but then again, they received none there when they were young.

In light of the contradictions and discontinuities with which all older people are confronted, it is evident that self-concept is an increasingly crucial factor in later life. Based on an understanding of who he or she "is," each person must mobilize his or her resources in order to either *adjust* or adjust *to* the changing expectations of others in a variety of social contexts. The very old have a vast store of experience that they can draw upon to either aid or inhibit their responses to the demands of new situations—situations in which their beliefs about themselves may not be recognized or accepted by others.

A major challenge for St. Petersburg's low-income elderly has been the need to adapt to racially mixed social situations. The white and black elderly have become co-recipients of a variety of social services, and are expected to participate as equals in programs such as congregate dining and adult day

1. Jasper C. Register has tested the assumption that young and middle-aged blacks have more favorable attitudes toward the elderly than do their white counterparts (1981:438-43). In one part of his survey, Register asked 3,446 whites and 619 blacks age eighteen and older whether they felt the elderly were: friendly and warm, physically attractive, bright and alert, good at getting things done, open-minded and adaptable, sexually active, and wise from experience. Respondents were grouped by age and, where possible, by socioeconomic status. Some 51.4 percent of young black respondents viewed the aged in a very positive light, as compared to 41.1 percent of whites; and 27 percent of young and middle-aged blacks held unfavorable views of aging and the aged, as compared to 38.6 percent of whites. See also Jackson (1980).

care. After a lifetime in segregated neighborhoods, the black elderly suddenly find themselves living in integrated high-rise apartment complexes. White retirees from the North, who have never interacted with blacks, find it easy to say they "aren't concerned with race"—until the first time their seat-mates at lunch are black members of their age cohort.

For the elderly black residents of St. Petersburg with whom I had contact, the expectation that they would eat, shop, and live with elderly whites represented a major ideological trans-formation. Memories of systematic degradation and abuse hov-ered at the forefront of consciousness. Informants spoke of ver-bal and physical threats, of being shunned in public places, of taking their children behind stores to urinate because no toilets for "coloreds" were provided. Visits to previously segregated landmarks inevitably provoked mental images of how things once were:

". . . in 1920 they had a big hurr'cane here. That was long in the time when you couldn't hardly get anythin to do here in the summertime. In 1926, I think it was, in 1926 they had another big storm here. Well, they used to have a boat they called the "Jennie B." It sunk. An down there where the Pier—they call it the Million Dollar Pier—well, it wasn' nothin like it is now. 'Cause this is the second time it's been built since then; the first was a small li'l ol place. An they didn' allow colored people to go down there unless they was workin.

"That's true. But when that big storm come, it tore up that place. An there was some big pine trees pretty close to the water; it blowed them down by the roots. An that Jennie B wharf boat, it sunk. An it was right funny; there was two ladies, two white ladies from the North, they went an looked at the trees all tore up, an that boat. An one of 'em says, 'You know what? I believed the colored people *prayed to their gods* for this to happen, 'cause they were too mean to 'em!'

"It tickled me—because she was talkin like the colored peo-ple's God weren't their God! I laughed till I cried."

[77]

Selena Harper, like many of her peers, had spent the better part of her life in a rented house owned by an absentee landlord. At ninety-two, she had outlived her entire family. Selena's house was finally torn down by the city; she took up residence on the fourteenth floor of a high-rise, denominationally sponsored apartment complex for the low-income elderly. Ironically, this apartment building overlooked the empty, unused lot where her rosebushes once bloomed.

In some ways, Selena's memories of the 1920s continued to have relevancy for her in the 1980s: "I don't think they done much changin," she said of her white neighbors in the high-rise complex. "They kinda put on a little bit . . . Plenty of 'em, right here in this building, got them same old ways about 'em."

At the same time, Selena had met many white friends through adult day care. As she was alone, they often invited her to visit their homes or to accompany them shopping or fishing. Selena enjoyed these outings. She felt strongly that a "modern" person, even at ninety-two, should be willing to accept social change:

"It ain't no use to keep thinkin on like that in your heart, 'cause that's done. Forgit 'bout the past an try for the future. That's the way I take it. Some of them [other blacks] go way back to slavery times. Talk about how they used to treat their old parents 'long in then. We can't help it 'bout what they done. What can you do about it?

"I look at a lot of (whites) right now. People what you used to go to the house, go there an work, and if you go you got to go to the *back* door. You go all *through* the house to work, front *an* back. Git ready to leave, you got to go back out that back door. An I look at 'em now, what I'm saying, they *glad* for you to come in the front door. That's right."

One can see that older black residents of St. Petersburg could find a great deal to be angry or bitter about. Yet in racially mixed settings I observed a strong willingness among black informants to converse with whites, make friends with those whites who seemed compatible, and ignore them otherwise. In other words, they seemed at ease.

Their white contemporaries, on the other hand, were often obsessed with the question of race. For some, the mere sight of a black person on the street or in a restaurant evoked expressions of anxiety and fear:

"The niggers, you see, they come from the part of town down off Ninth Street on the south side. And then they come from the other way, Methodist Town, and that's *all* niggers. And you'd think they own the place . . .

"They got into my bag, stole my billfold. I got 'em, two nigger boys. Somebody said, 'You better call the police.' I said, 'What for? They're not gonna do anything with 'em if they catch 'em.'"

These comments were offered by a retired woman from Michigan whom I met in a downtown St. Petersburg restaurant. Like most such "unsolicited testimonies," this one began with a public reference; she asked if I had read about a recent racial incident that took place during a parade. When I said no, she described it with relish, used it to lead into a personal incident, and then proceeded to vent her negative feelings about blacks in general.

A similar pattern emerged during a discussion with a white informant about nursing homes:

"My brother is in a rest home in Sarasota. This one is run by the Mennonites, and they are fine people. The staff is all white people. Of course, most of the homes around here have all Negroes working in them. You didn't know *that*, did you? Well, they're not good to the people."

Why is it that the black elderly, despite their painful memories, seemed willing to negotiate new relationships with whites, while white retirees became increasingly reluctant to extend recognition to their black contemporaries? To approach this complicated question, it is necessary to review the patterns of employment, residence, and kin-based interaction among

[79]

the members of each group. These factors should not be regarded as isolated variables amenable to comparison with standard models for adult role engagement, but as interdependent
components of the experience of social aging.

Kin-Based Interactions

School busing and equal opportunity employment are too
"new" to have had direct impact on the lives of my black informants. Yet they had ample opportunity to observe and evaluate the impact of these changes on the lives of their children,
grandchildren, and great-grandchildren. Black informants often made comparisons between their own childhood experiences and the life-styles of younger kin. This cross-generational
perspective provided both a model for structuring their own interactions with whites and a vehicle for "making sense" of the
transition between past and present.

"An then one time, I don' know whether the mens was guilty
or not. But it was people that used to work for 'em lived up the
Coastline Railroad there, right 'side the railroad. An he hired a
lot of people, you know, to work. It was every man that they
knowed worked for them people, they arrested them. An there
was two worked there, they said them an the boss man had a
fallin out about diggin post holes. One was named Evans, an I
forgot what t'other was named—it'll come to me after a while.
An they had, oh I don' know, they had the jail *full* of people
they arrested. One man was in the jail for stealin oranges an
grapefruits.

"Now this is the truth: they took them mens an lynched 'em.
One of 'em. T'other was hung, in Tampa. They claimed they
kilt the man (the railroad boss) and the wo— the lady [his
wife]. Out of all them people, just them two, they kilt 'em. Kilt
one, you know what I mean, *lynched* him. In the street. Right
on Second Avenue South. Ninth Street and Second Avenue,

there's a telephone—telegram—pole sittin there. 'Course it's
not the pole that was there then, 'cause after they did that they
took that pole down. Brought him from the li'l jail, from downtown, to Second Avenue South. They say he was dead when he
got down there. Swung 'em up on that telephone pole, an shot
'em to death. Shot 'em to *pieces;* they say he was already dead
'cause they had done shot him, an kicked him, an beat him up.
Don' know whether he did what they say or not.

"Yeah, that was a *lynch* mob. Ku Klux Klans 'n things. That
was a terr'ble time here in St. Petersburg. They didn't allow
the colored people to have a light in their house. Couldn't open
the door, couldn't make a sound or no kind of . . . Well, after
they lynched him, that was at night, the next day somebody
come through. I don' know who it was, but whoever it was they
come through town and they say: 'The colored people say last
night was your night, but tonight's gonna be theirs.'

"Man, you talk about [white] people gettin outa town! Goin
all out; some went to Tampa 'n some went other places, 'n
some went as far out as they could get, like Pass-a-Grille,[2]
places like that. But that wasn' true. Whoever done that just
did it for meanness, I reckon, or devilment.

"You see, they hurt the town when they did that, 'cause a lot
of the touristers were here. It was in the winter time. A lot of
them touristers just picked up—just about *all* of them—just
picked up an *left*. It was a long time 'fore they started to comin
back here in the winter. They see where they had hurt theirselves by lynchin that man like that. You know, right on the
street, where everybody's passin. They saw where they had
hurt theirselves by doin that, an they haven't did it anymore
since, as I know of. An I think I would of known it if it had a
happened, because I been here all that time."

Selena Harper's memory of a 1914 lynching—corroborated
by other informants—was one of many stories used by St.

2. A barrier island beach community, about eight miles from downtown St.
Petersburg. In 1914, it was accessible only by boat (Hurley 1977).

Petersburg's black elderly to point up the contrast between past and present. Such experiences marked them as survivors, and they were recognized and respected as such by younger family members. At the same time, most of them realized that the world was different for their grandchildren, and, by extension, for themselves as well.

The majority of my white informants did not live in close proximity to younger relatives. They generally acquired information about racial issues from the news media and from stories related by friends and kin in northern cities. Needless to say, when a story about race made the news, it was usually "bad news," and observations made by northern relatives were often irrelevant to the issue of integration in Florida. For most of the white informants, integration remained an abstract topic of debate and a matter of personal choice. Some considered it a welcome and long-overdue change; others viewed it as an abrupt and discontinuous transformation of the status quo. Either way, the choice to maximize or minimize contact with blacks remained grounded in past experience and in a pre-existing system of values and beliefs. Thus, unlike the black elderly, who based their assessment of current trends on a temporal perspective that stretched unbroken from early childhood in the South through the experiences of grandchildren and great-grandchildren, older whites were often thrown back upon the past as the primary source of inspiration to guide their encounters with blacks.

Residency

According to a local survey conducted by the city's Management Improvement Department in 1975, "Most residents interviewed have lived in St. Petersburg more than a year. Nonwhites seem particularly familiar with the City, with 77%

9. After church

10. Williams Park

11. Band concert, Williams Park

12. Band shell area, Williams Park

13. First Avenue N. between Fourth and Fifth Streets

14. Recycling aluminum cans, downtown

claiming a five year residency (versus only 71% of whites)." The steady migration of retired northerners to Florida contributed significantly to the shorter duration of residency observed among the white elderly. Even more significant, however, was the uncharted mobility of older residents *within* the city. The well-to-do retiree who purchased a home or condominium could expect to remain in that location for many years. The low-income retiree, on the other hand, often gravitated to the downtown rental district. He or she could expect to move frequently.

My own next-door neighbors, a retired couple in their early seventies, changed residence three times during the year that I knew them. (They were contemplating a fourth move when I left the neighborhood.) On short notice, they would pack up their belongings in a "borrowed" shopping cart and transfer them to another furnished apartment. After the first move, I kept notes on their reasons: "The refrigerator and heater don't work right so our electric bills are too high." "There are hippies and drug pushers in the house across the street." "The old lady on the other side of the house watches us all the time; I hate nosy neighbors."

This rootless life-style was common among my white informants. Nevertheless, many did maintain the loose-knit, "diffuse-cluster" social support networks described by Sokolovsky and Cohen (1981, 1983) for inner-city, single-room occupancy hotel dwellers (few were as poor, however). They saw each other on a regular basis in city parks, downtown cafeterias or congregate dining sites, and stores.

Except when forced to move by eminent domain or a disastrous reduction in income, older black informants were likely to stay in the same neighborhoods for many years. Most had migrated to St. Petersburg at a relatively young age and remained to work and raise families. Thus their contacts with neighbors tended to be much more stable and frequent. When they did move to a low-income project for the elderly or to the home of a younger relative, ties with old friends were maintained through the church, through contact among their extended families and the extended families of their friends, and, of course, by telephone.

Interaction with relatives and neighbors and the selective nature of access to information could thus be regarded as primary contributing factors in the formation of attitudes about race—or about any subject, for that matter. Within a given community, informal exchanges between individuals formed a rhetorical chain that helped transform private experience into shared, "public" knowledge. When intergenerational bonds were strong, as they were in St. Petersburg's black community, experiences rooted in the past were continually reworked in light of more recent knowledge. When both community and intergenerational bonds were weak, as they were for many low-income white retirees, the individual was left with few guides to negotiate the contradictions between past and present.

Employment

Sigmund Freud wrote in *Civilization and Its Discontents:* "No other technique for the conduct of life attaches the individual so firmly to reality as laying emphasis on work; for his work at least gives him a secure place in a portion of reality, in the human community" (1962:27f). Just as retirement contributed to the estrangement of some white elderly from the wider community, work provided the black elderly with a variety of insights into the changing urban milieu. In 1970, when the majority of my informants were already past the traditional retirement age, 10.4 percent of men age sixty-five and older and 5.4 of women of this age in Pinellas County were considered active members of the labor force. Within this group, the figures were 35 percent for black men and 27.6 percent for black women (Osterbind 1976:53). These statistics take on additional significance when considered in relation to state-wide estimates of income sources for the population age sixty-five and older (see Figure 1).

The black elderly, more actively engaged in work, were also more dependent upon earnings than were their white counterparts. Since a majority of my own black informants were over seventy-five, few of them worked outside the home. Yet, like other members of St. Petersburg's black community, many had continued to work well past the age of sixty-five. Most black female informants had spent their working lives as domestics or restaurant workers; most men, after a stint at construction work, had settled into independent businesses within their extended neighborhoods. Some had never participated in the Social Security system. "Mandatory retirement" occurred when the individual was no longer phsysically able to work.

While independent employment freed the black aged from forced retirement, it often obligated them to continue working as long as possible, even to the detriment of their health. Those who had been engaged as domestics in white homes often realized too late that their employers had never contributed to Social Security on their behalf, leaving them ineligible for benefits or pensions. Since few had earned enough to accumulate savings during their most active years, the prospect of retirement raised the spectre of "going on the welfare." This was regarded as a last resort at best, and as a bitter commentary on the low value bestowed upon black labor. In the words of one seventy-five-year-old recipient of public assistance: "I worked hard [for whites] all the time. Did the laundry, cooked, cleaned, took care of the children—even put them to bed. And now, I got nothing to show for it."

Stories about work were particularly significant for my informants; the work situation held serious implications for the development of identity and the achievement of mutual recognition. Black informants agreed that their employers did not

[91]

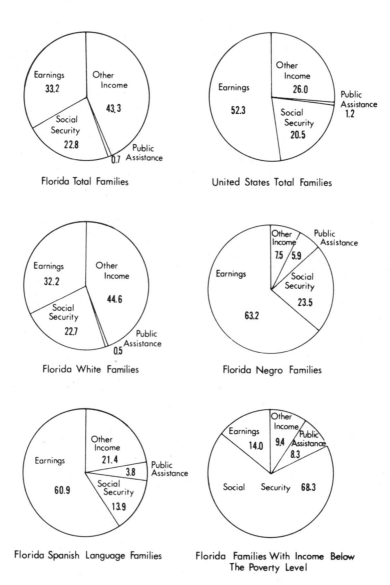

Figure 1. Income sources of families with head aged sixty-five and over

"know" them, did not treat them as peers who shared their value system. On the other hand, they felt secure in their understanding of whites and white motives.

One retired housekeeper told me that her employers would sometimes leave money between the pages of magazines or in other more conspicuous places to discover whether or not she would steal. When she found money, she would either leave it in place or call an employer's attention to it. Finally, in exasperation, she said to one family: "You always leavin money around to see will I steal. Well, the next time I find somethin, I'm gonna keep it." They got the point.[3]

Most black elderly informants had worked long and hard for shockingly low wages. As a result, few enjoyed any cushion against illness, a pattern that had persisted into their retirement years. Consider this incident, related by a subject during a discussion of what life in St. Petersburg was like during the Great Depression:

"Came a time when my mother 'n sister was sick . . . We didn' have any money left and there was no groceries in the house. I didn' know what to do or where the money would be comin from. So that night I got down on my knees and prayed to the Lord that He would show me the way to get a little somethin to take care of my mother 'n sister. Well, the next day, a man whose washin I used to do sometimes brought me some clothes. He had been to fishin, and in the pants he had wore I found seven dollars. Now I never did do any stealin, but I took that seven dollars and carried it right on to George's —you know, the little store I was tellin you about—and spent all of it on groceries. My mother 'n sister was too sick to eat lots of foods, so I bought a lot of soup that they liked.

---

3. Liebow (1967) commented on the structure established by white employers in their dealings with black workers in marginal jobs. He noted that black workers were often deliberately underpaid, with the expectation that they would inevitably steal a certain amount of money or goods. The workers themselves were then forced to fulfill this expectation in order to achieve a living wage.

"Later on, when they got better, I told them about it. I said, 'Remember all that good soup you had when you was sick?' They said yes. 'Well,' I said, 'I found some money in a man's pants I was washin, and I spent it all on groceries.' My mother said that was bad, but I said it was bad to be hungry. I prayed to the Lord, and I figure that money was His blessin."

White retirees spent their working years in other states, under different conditions. Those who sought to re-enter the work force in St. Petersburg found marginal employment at best. Many sought part-time positions, but jobs were scarce and employers were inclined to pass them over in favor of younger workers. This was difficult for those in their early sixties, particularly women, who were too young for Social Security but too old to appeal to potential employers.

One such woman was Adrienne Moore, aide-receptionist for a local nonprofit organization. Adrienne was an outgoing, attractive woman, successful in her job and highly rated by her employer and co-workers. When Adrienne's husband lost *his* job, however, she felt compelled to resign from this low-wage position in order to seek work elsewhere. Adrienne spent several frustrating months going from one interview to another: "No matter how well qualified I am, they take one look and say no. Today I was passed over again; the job went to a nineteen-year-old girl with absolutely no experience."

Even among those low-income white elderly who did work and thus came in contact with a wider social community, efforts to expand work-based associations with blacks into personal friendships were sometimes subjected to adverse peer pressure. Lois Martin, a midwesterner in her mid-sixties, related this experience:

"There was a colored girl that stayed at our hotel where I worked, that's the one at Second and Central. And, ah, she was kind to me and I was kind to her. . . . And God Almighty— when they saw me walking in there they'd say, 'Lois, we saw you sitting with a colored girl.' I said, 'So what?' And they said, 'Well, my God!'

"Everybody's eyes went that big in the place when I walked in with her. Well, we even danced together. . . . They said, 'My God, Lois, she's *colored!*'

"I said, 'I don't care what race, or creed, or religion a person is; they're all God's children, right?' . . . You bet they are!"

To assess the validity of any interpretive model in the study of adult behavior, one must consider how it utilizes the subject's past experience in predicting that person's present and future identity. All people must base their actions on the knowledge and experience that are already theirs. Beliefs, attitudes, and expectations formed throughout the course of the life cycle will continue to influence behavior in the ongoing present. Yet the past is not enough. It is evident that the aging individual cannot maintain recognition through use of the faded social photograph, particularly when changes in employment status, income, and kin networks have rendered the predominant "features" unrecognizable.

When dealing with the very old, one must be particularly careful to tread a fine line between synchrony and diachrony. Psychoanalytic models draw heavily on the *formative influence* of the past, thus predicting a present and future in which there is little room for true adaptation to change. Such models produce synchronic distortion (reduction), or what Burke has termed a "temporizing of essence."[4] Strict adherence to the developmental model would oblige one to assume that the adult personality is fully formed and relatively impervious to change. The structural rigidity of such a model can inhibit the

---

4. "Because of the pun whereby the logically prior can be expressed in terms of the temporally prior, and v.v., the ways of transcendence, in aiming at the discovery of *essential* motives, may often take the historicist form of symbolic *regression*. That is, if one is seeking for the 'essence' of motives, one can only express such a search in the temporal terms of imaginative literature as a process of 'going back.' And conversely, one given to retrospect, as Proust in his 'remembrance of things past,' may conceptualize his concern as a search for 'essence.'

"This double vocabulary for the expression of essence is, I think, a basic factor to be watched continually if one would know how to translate back and forth between logical and temporal vocabularies" (1969:430).

attempt to understand the effects of changing cultural demands on the aging individual's self-conception. Those who adapt well to radically altered definitions of who they are do so by assimilating and integrating a variety of new experiences, a fact that has received scant attention in the literature on the psychology of aging.

The weaknesses of the psychologist's synchronic model are counterbalanced by the diachronic weakness of role theory in sociological and traditional ethnographic description. Role theory, when applied literally to the elderly, draws upon the past as a *measure of peak involvement*, thus predicting a present and future that are comparatively devoid of opportunities for social recognition. Such a model does provide a functional outline of the cultural construction of old age—the means by which society "acts upon" the older person over time. Yet this one-sided perspective cannot by itself provide an understanding of the broad spectrum of individual response to changes in role expectation.

Unfortunately, these paradigms sometimes mirror the perspective of the investigator rather than the lives of his or her subjects. Such "compensatory" models for the study of aging often demean the experience of informants, offering little insight into the significant life changes that can be—and are—accomplished very late in life. These changes can often be traced directly to the problem of identity orientation and the older person's need to achieve mutual recognition vis-à-vis others. I have presented one aspect of this concern: the establishment of recognition between two groups of older people where none had existed before. There are many others. Only a truly nonfinite, processual model can fully recognize the older person's attempts to maintain social equilibrium and the means employed to achieve it.

PART TWO

Social Policy and the Reality of Aging

It's time we tried to keep them here, and make it attractive. Now, they are going to have to afford it. It's not up to the government to pay for them to do that. And if they can't afford it, then they will be replaced with people who can. . . . An eighty-eight-year-old lady can't expect things to stay the same just for her. They dislike change. We do know that very clearly.

downtown St. Petersburg businessman

[4]

Housing

Everybody writes about housing, but no one gives you the choice. To me, housing is a storage warehouse for the undertakers. They can't bury us all at once, so they pick us off one at a time. Another thing I call it, another name: "The House of Mourning." Before one dies and we mourn this one, another one dies. That's just a part of life; why can't we have a choice? Why can't we say, "You want to go into low-cost housing, fine. But if I don't, give me the cash and I can live anywhere I want with dignity and self-respect." It's high time that we stopped all this shoving us into these storage warehouses.

Max Friedson, age seventy-seven

The study of aging is much more than an academic debate carried on among a limited group of social scientists. Just as the presentation and widespread acceptance of the Moynihan report (1965) has had long-term and, as it happens, controversial effects on the planning of social policy with regard to the black family, so the current theses advanced in the field of aging have exercised and will continue to exercise considerable influence over the planning and enactment of policy decisions with regard to the aged.

Unfortunately for all concerned, few have risen from among the ranks of the elderly to serve as spokespersons and critics of current policy and the research findings upon which it is based.[1] Most have assumed that the aged in need of social ser-

1. Maggie Kuhn and the Philadelphia-based Gray Panthers are notable exceptions.

vices are too uneducated, uninterested, or "disengaged" to examine what is said about them and to influence the direction of future thinking. It may be, however, that we have not presented our findings in forms that are *accessible* to the old.

The majority of my informants did not know what the word "gerontology" meant. The presence of a researcher who was interested in their problems and sought to understand them was an intriguing but unfamiliar idea. They were amazed to discover that the government offered grants for the study of old people, and that "theories" about aging existed. It is significant to note that these low-income elderly were the same people for whom most of the social service programs had been formulated. While social workers and service agencies constituted a primary influence in their lives, they remained unaware of the motivating principles behind the services offered to them.

In the case of the sociological study of the black family, it was only when black scholars themselves rose to refute the assumptions upon which theoretical models were based that scientific research became more self-reflexive. Until that time, the outside investigator was not called upon to re-examine the relationship between *a priori* assumptions about blacks and the actual data collected. Methodology and theory "made sense" because they remained internal to a pre-established system of stereotyped beliefs.

This tautological approach has been equally evident in the study of aging. The researcher arrives in the field armed with a concrete definition of "old age." He or she then employs a methodological approach that is geared to substantiate this definition with selectively gathered "empirical" data. Such data are used to reinforce the existing superstructure of policy and legislation, which in turn helps to maintain the elderly within the limits of culturally constructed old age.

During the laissez-faire late 1950s, for instance, Elaine Cumming and William Henry suggested that "disengagement" from social relations was a natural adaptation to the aging process

(1961). Observing that the frequency of social interactions decreased with advanced age, these authors postulated that an underlying psychodynamic led the older person to become increasingly self-absorbed; at the same time, society began to release its hold on the individual. In essence, the older person and society "agreed to disagree."

The disengagement theory generated a storm of protest among other researchers, most notably the proponents of the diametrically opposed "activity" theory (Maddox 1964), and also prompted the attempt to seek a middle ground (Havighurst et al. 1968). On a practical level, the concept of disengagement fell into disfavor during the mid-1960s because federal policy dictated that money and manpower, channeled through Older Americans Act programs, should be directed toward helping the elderly maintain activity, independence, and engagement in their communities. For political purposes, disengagement proved an unpopular notion.

Efforts to keep the elderly "engaged" proved quite expensive, however. At the same time that the Reagan administration began cutting back on community programs for the aged, researchers began rethinking their approach to the "problems" of growing old. Age-homogeneous communities, or what Friedson called "warehouses for the undertakers,"[2] began to look less like ghettos for the victims of social and economic ageism and more like reasonable, even creative alternatives to participation in the wider community. Keith has argued persuasively that older people adapt well to such settings, where adult role losses are replaced by a sense of collective equality among members of an age cohort (1982, 1983).

Age-homogeneous communities are a boon for researchers; they offer a whole new set of social roles to quantify, chart, and evaluate. They are also a boon for public and private develop-

2. Friedson favored instead the Section 8 housing program, which allowed qualified recipients to receive rent subsidies for housing they selected on their own, subject to approval by the administering agency.

ers, who find a ready market in those who have accepted the notion that the aged are happier—not to mention safer —among their own kind. Among the elderly themselves, however, age-homogeneous communities have received mixed reviews. It can safely be said that older people are remarkably adept at adapting to the conditions set for them by society. Whether they are happy or not is another question.

Throughout the course of my research I have been confronted again and again with the visible effects of social planning based on a limited, stereotyped assessment of needs and expectations. If significant numbers of older people were to present their true opinions as forcefully as Max Friedson, the odds for upgrading current living conditions for the elderly would improve considerably. Not everyone is born to be a public speaker, of course, and advocates like Friedson and Maggie Kuhn of the Gray Panthers emanate charismatic qualities all their own. Yet the differences between these advocates and my informants were based as much in the reality of daily living as in the intangible components of personality. One can assume that if Friedson and Kuhn were to be turned out of their homes suddenly by angry landlords who failed to appreciate their outspokenness, each would have numerous alternatives to living in a nursing home. The majority of my informants, however, believed they were totally at the mercy of landlords, social workers, and the city itself. They were afraid; they remained silent. Most often, their silence was taken as acquiescence.

Relocation

Laurene Garson moved to St. Petersburg in 1909, when job prospects were good for a young black woman seeking a position as a restaurant cook. In 1916 she rented a small, tin-roofed house "built out of all good heart wood. You can't get that kind of lumber no more." In 1923 Laurene's landlord brought in a mule team and hauled her house from its original location to the segregated Gas Plant neighborhood. Laurene went with it. She stayed on to raise a family, plant shrubs and bushes, and develop an extended support network in her neighborhood.

In 1980, ninety-four-year-old Laurene still chopped wood for the stove where she did all her cooking with groceries she carried home from the store on foot. She kept track of a variety of younger friends and relatives, who were always ready to lend a hand when something needed fixing: "A drapery rod fell down in my kitchen the other day. One of the young fellows came by and put it up for me. He said I was *too old* to be climbing up on chairs." She paused for emphasis. "Maybe he was right," she added with a wry smile.

Laurene's neighborhood was considered "incredibly bad as slum conditions go" by the business community. A new interstate highway overpass exposed it to the full scrutiny of tourists—not the type of image the city fathers favored. They reasoned that they would be doing the residents a favor to tear it down. Besides, they wanted the land for an industrial park and a baseball stadium.

Seventy of the Gas Plant's eight hundred residents signed a petition in favor of relocation. The rest remained curiously silent. For the young, relocation meant a fresh start. For the old, it meant goodbye to friendly neighbors, neighborhood stores, a ride to church—the small, well-earned conveniences that make independent living possible at eighty or ninety. The neighbors of a 105-year-old man worried about his future. Would his new neighbors cook his meals, clean his house, and do his laundry, as his old neighbors had done? Would relocation officials "notice" that he couldn't take care of himself and pack him off to a nursing home?

"This house was bought and sold seven times since I've been in it. You know I hate to move," said Laurene. "Got to go, though, and don't know where we're going. Might be on a dark street, or in a rough place. You know, some places in town are *very* rough. Might be so noisy I can't make it."

[103]

The city dispatched Laurene (very gently, of course) to a high-rise complex for the low-income elderly. Always gracious, she announced that she loved it there, that she had been "crazy" to resist the move. At the same time, though, she increased her visits to the adult day care center from two days a week to five. Before, she had always been "too busy." Now there were no weeds to battle, no wood to chop, no need to keep an eye out for bargains at the corner store. For a woman who took pride in making her own way, there was nothing left to do at all.

Low-Income Housing

Whether one thrives or languishes in a high-rise housing project depends largely on one's personal history and to what extent relocation constitutes a severing of significant ties. When the move is voluntary, as it was for the majority of my white informants, it often means freedom from anxiety about the whims of avaricious or capricious landlords. While the residents of low-income housing whom I talked to often expressed regret at the loss of their former homes, they remained surrounded by their own possessions and, for the most part, were able to maintain the privacy and dignity of independent living. For the first time in years, many informants found themselves in apartments that were truly *theirs*—at least until such time as failing health might make it impossible for them to survive without assistance.

This possibility generated its own anxiety, of course; I heard several stories about seriously ill or disabled people who went to great lengths to hide their problems from housing project administrators. This is essentially no different, however, from the situation of aging private homeowners who attempt to bolster their waning strength for the benefit of neighbors and kin. In either case, the fault lies less with *where* the person lives than with the paucity of his or her alternatives in times of need.

Several of my principal informants lived in Graham Park and John Knox Apartments, two low-income, high-rise complexes located within a few blocks of each other in downtown St. Petersburg. Graham Park was a federally sponsored project; John Knox was built by the Presbyterian Homes and Housing Foundation of Florida. Resident populations of these complexes were interchangeable with regard to background and income; the final choice of where to live was often determined by where one stood on the waiting lists. As the organization and overall atmosphere of both were quite similar, I shall consider them together.

Back in 1975, informants agreed that the best thing about living in these high-rise complexes was their location. Both were located on or near major bus routes. For the relatively hearty, both were within walking distance of the Central Avenue retail stores and restaurants. Best of all, both were just a stone's throw away from Webb's City, "World's Most Unusual Drug Store."

Webb's City began in the 1920s as a hole-in-the-wall pharmacy run by James Earl "Doc" Webb, an outgoing young businessman with a flair for the dramatic. He sold discounted merchandise directly from boxcars; he sponsored beauty contests; and he turned a small drugstore into a homegrown Florida tourist attraction.

Webb's expanded over the years to cover several city blocks. Its distinctive, rambling buildings housed the only supermarket in downtown St. Petersburg, plus a department store, furniture store, drug store, restaurant, bakery, dry cleaning plant, barber shop, beauty salon, gasoline station, automotive store, plant nursery, newspaper stand, post office substation, ice cream shop, shoe store and repair shop, check cashing service, and souvenir stand—to name just a few of the shopping complex's seventy-seven businesses. There were indoor benches where tired shoppers could rest their feet, and a variety of quaint amusements, including an assortment of trained chickens, ducks, and rabbits that performed tricks for a dime. In an

[105]

era of advertising hyperbole, Webb's claim to uniqueness was an understatement.

In the minds of St. Petersburg's younger residents, Webb's was a nagging anachronism, a monument to the "green bench" days. Although it was convenient and inexpensive, most younger people preferred to shop elsewhere, *anywhere* else. "Too many old people there." "It's too depressing." "Too slow, with all those old folks crowding up the aisles."

For the low-income residents of John Knox and Graham Park, Webb's City was a lifeline. It often made the difference between independence and social indebtedness, a decent meal and malnutrition, a few extra pennies and an empty pocketbook. Here the elderly could shop for supplies by the day, instead of calling on friends and relatives with cars to haul a week's groceries from one of the suburban supermarkets. (Many older people wheeled Webb's City shopping carts home, but no one seemed to mind—they always brought them back.) Bored with eating alone, the single person could enjoy a decent breakfast or lunch in the company of others. For the very poor and for those men who did not know how to cook, one meal a day at Webb's was often *all* they ate. "I try to time it so I come in here in the middle of the day," one lady told me. "Then I go to bed early, so I'm not real hungry until the next day."

Webb's went out of business in 1979. The city of St. Petersburg purchased the complex; the main building was demolished in 1984. "Webb's City's closing is probably a good thing," said a downtown banker. "It can now be modernized and be a contributing taxpayer. The Webb's City concept? The world passed it by."

And with it, the world passed by hundreds of high-rise apartment dwellers who were stranded with no drugstore, no supermarket, no restaurant. "Ain't nothing you can get up here," said a Graham Park informant. "It's completely blacked out. There's no place to get something to eat, nowhere to buy food, the postal needs and everything. I don't see how we can get along."

"If the city would make up its mind to give things back to the elderly, they'd have no problems," said one retiree who had fought hard to convince the business community that Webb's should be kept alive. "They're not interested. . . . If you have a city that tears down buildings and puts in parking lots, that's the end in that area."

I believe that location alone distinguished John Knox and Graham Park from the "houses of mourning" described by elderly advocate Max Friedson. In fact, most of the private retirement complexes I visited *did* fit that description. These were located in relatively isolated areas, well removed from the mainstream of activity and accessible only by car. They constituted self-contained social units; residents were forced to rely exclusively on each other and on "activity directors" to fulfill both physical and social needs. While the low-income residents of John Knox and Graham Park enjoyed much less financial independence than did their middle-income contemporaries, they were initially free to shop unassisted and to participate in age-integrated activities. Thus the move to one of these projects was much less disruptive than the move to a planned community or suburban condominium.

The location of John Knox and Graham Park was particularly significant for black residents of these units. Both projects were built in a traditionally desegregated section of the business district. As a result, friends and kin of minority residents could visit freely without feeling self-conscious and without being exposed to resentment from white homeowners in the area. At the same time, the black elderly themselves were able to retain outward mobility. Sadly, this would not have been possible had the housing projects been located just a few blocks farther east.[3] The black and white elderly had traditionally mingled in

3. The Sunshine Center, St. Petersburg's multiservice facility for the elderly, was constructed just four blocks east of John Knox Apartments in the "Mirror

Webb's City and other retail stores surrounding the projects. The existence of integrated shopping in this neighborhood helped to establish a precedent for behavior among complex residents, most of whom had never lived in integrated housing before.

State-Supported Facilities for the Dependent Elderly

For the reasonably healthy older person, placement in an age-segregated housing project did not require the intervention of a social worker. Those elderly who could not see to their own physical needs were assigned to a variety of state "protective care" facilities. Placement in the state system involved the establishment of three long-term relationships: applicant/social worker, applicant/boarding home owner, and applicant/co-residents of the living facility. Once formed, these relationships often constituted an oppressive network from which older people were powerless to extricate themselves. There was a basic, if unintended, contradiction between the motives of "protective" service policies and the need for self-determination among the poor and disabled.

Matthew Parsons was born in 1910, the only child of a poor Alabama family. Matthew, who was blind, had received little formal education, but he had absorbed many impressions and ideas through travel. He was very talented as a singer in the traditional Delta blues style, and had traveled extensively over the years playing the guitar and supplementing his income

---

Lake" area, which contains one of the highest concentrations of white retirees. Presumably intended for use by *all* older downtown residents, the facility's location in a traditionally segregated neighborhood has thwarted attempts by city Office on Aging staff to attract the black elderly. Several years after the construction of the Sunshine Center, the city built another multiservice facility in an all-black neighborhood.

with a variety of odd jobs. Matthew had passed through St. Petersburg many times "when the railroad stopped right downtown." He did not expect to stay when he returned once again in search of work, but times were slow in the music business and a downtown cafeteria offered him a steady job washing dishes. He worked five years at the cafeteria, living in a rented room and commuting to work by bus. Failing health and "bad nerves" forced him to retire at age sixty-four.

Matthew applied for Supplemental Security Income, to which he was entitled as a disabled person. Unfortunately, the payments were not enough for him to continue his longstanding, informal contract with his landlady, who cooked his meals and looked after his clothes. Instead, he was assigned a social worker by the Florida Department of Health and Rehabilitative Services. This agency decided Matthew should be placed in one of the many boarding homes that were licensed to accept state clients.[4]

Matthew had been living in this boarding home for seventeen months when I first met him at an adult day care center in 1975. He was quite communicative but focused his remarks almost exclusively on the past, describing in great detail his life on the road. I could not help noticing that his clothing was very unkempt and that most of his shirts seemed several sizes too large. When he mentioned that he had no spending money, I began to question him casually about the boarding home and the services provided for him. At that point, Matthew became evasive; he feigned "forgetfulness" and nervously attempted to change the subject as quickly as possible.

I began to spend several hours a week with Matthew at the adult center, and eventually he told me something of his home situation. He was always very guarded, though, and would only speak about it after I had gone through the ritual of swearing

---

4. The State of Florida has significantly upgraded the specifications governing these boarding homes, which are now known as adult congregate living facilities.

that I would not repeat what he said to anyone. I did, however, take notes:

1. Shares a room with a sick man he does not know well. This man is "off his head" (delirious). "Should be in the hospital." Keeps Matthew awake at night.

2. No control over his own money. SSI payments have not been sufficiently explained to him. Does not know the amount of his check. Landlady keeps his money, gives him $2 per week.[5]

3. Wears a heavy overcoat to the day care center even on warm days for fear that it will be stolen. At home many small personal items have been taken and his complaints about this denied or ignored. Clothing given to him at the center is rarely seen again.

4. Has complained to his social worker, who repeated his confidential statements to the landlady. She became very angry and accused him of exaggeration and untruthfulness. He felt that his action served to place him in an even more compromising position.

5. Matthew is not allowed to receive visitors at home.

6. Matthew is not allowed to place or receive phone calls.

Matthew and I discussed the possibility of bringing these grievances to the attention of the day care center staff, whom he trusted. Once again, he became very fearful. He stipulated that he would talk to them if it could be arranged for him to move away from the boarding home on the same day the landlady was informed of his dissatisfaction. Otherwise, he said, he would be "afraid to spend the night." When the manager of the center did approach him, he denied everything he had told me.

A few months later, several participants at the day care center contracted influenza. One man who lived alone died at home before he could tell anyone that he needed to see a doctor. Anticipating that other participants might lack access to

5. At the time, state welfare clients were entitled to a personal spending allowance of twenty-five dollars per month.

medical care, the center's nurse began to check on absent people. Matthew had been out sick for about three weeks, so she made an appointment with his doctor. My husband and I agreed to provide his transportation. Shortly after the appointment had been made, the nurse received an angry call from Matthew's landlady. She said Matthew was being "taken care of" and that his social worker planned to take him to the doctor. The nurse and I agreed that it would be a good idea for me to visit Matthew anyway.

My initial visit to Matthew's run-down boarding home was the single most disturbing experience I have had—before or since—in eleven years of working with older people.

We were met at the door by an irate housekeeper, who informed us that Mr. Parsons could not leave the premises without the landlady's permission. She was not at home, so we decided to wait. We were ushered into a disorderly living room where we settled down on a couple of unsteady, plastic-covered chairs. A television set blared loudly from one corner. The room was crowded with people of all ages, all in varying states of personal disarray. Several of the younger ones appeared to be brain-damaged. A strong smell of dirt and urine permeated the air.

I insisted that Matthew be called down from his room, as we were denied permission to go upstairs. He had a terrible hacking cough and seemed to be running a high fever. He had never been informed of the doctor's appointment, but now expressed a strong desire to keep it. Once again, we were told that he could not leave without the landlady's permission.

The landlady was almost beside herself when she returned to find us waiting for her. She launched into a lengthy diatribe against us, the adult center, and most particularly Matthew himself. She accused him of "faking," "lying," and trying to stir up trouble by involving outsiders in boarding home affairs. Between spasms of coughing, Matthew protested weakly that we were his friends and that he really *did* need to get some medi-

[111]

cine. "Go ahead," she said finally, "and you needn't come back, either, big a liar as you are." Matthew was diagnosed as suffering from pneumonia.

Incensed by this incident, I brought my observations to the attention of Matthew's social worker. She replied coldly that she had always enjoyed "a good working relationship" with the owner of the boarding home. Then she turned to a discussion of Matthew himself, describing him as a pathological liar who was badly in need of mental health counseling. She substantiated this assessment by pointing out that he had complained before, then denied what he had said when it came to a confrontation. I asked if she had ever wondered why Matthew was so intimidated by his surroundings and by those in authority. She promised to speak with the landlady again and to investigate alternative living situations for Matthew. Nothing came of it.

I returned many times to visit this boarding home. At first I was met with great resistance; the landlady told me I could not set foot on the premises without her express permission. The reasons for her guarded attitude soon became obvious. I saw one resident strike another; the landlady just laughed until she realized that I was watching. I heard a brain-damaged resident being beaten for refusing to eat her supper. I watched the gradual deterioration of an elderly man who had once been a participant at the day care center; he ambled back and forth on the front porch in urine-soaked trousers. I also observed that there was only one functioning toilet for the thirteen or more people who lived in the boarding home. The owner did not live there herself and the residents—all blind, mentally deficient, or in wheelchairs—were left unattended at night. (Matthew and some of the other boarders told me that prostitutes and their drunken clients sometimes used the premises after hours.) As the residents were in a state of complete financial dependency, I was often asked for gifts of small change, snack foods, and soap.

Throughout all of this Matthew remained in a deep depression. He began to speak openly of suicide. He also considered the possibility of entering a nursing home as the only alternative to his present situation.

Eventually a *St. Petersburg Times* reporter happened to meet Matthew at the adult center. A lengthy interview appeared in the *Times*, bringing Matthew to the attention of musicians and blues enthusiasts. Soon afterward his social worker arranged for him to move to an adult foster care home.

Here Matthew's health and demeanor underwent a drastic, immediate transformation. With a guitar bought for him through a benefit fund-raiser, he began performing in public again. He became a favorite at the annual Florida Folk Festival and at blues clubs in the St. Petersburg area. Folklorists came from as far away as South Carolina to interview him and to record his music. His foster family enjoyed dressing him up for his concerts and welcomed the musicians who came to visit him. Matthew remained active in the local music scene until a few months before his death from a heart attack in late 1981.

The case of Matthew Parsons is not intended to serve as a basis for extrapolation about the quality of "congregate living" facilities and foster care. Many such programs are excellent; Matthew experienced both the best and the worst. Efforts are made to see that living environments for the dependent elderly conform to established state guidelines; the common goal is to provide positive alternatives to nursing home placement for older people who cannot continue to function in the community without assistance. Yet on a qualitative level, there can be no true standardization. By their very nature, these living environments are as varied as the personalities and circumstances of those who administer them.

All "protective" social service programs share the potential to produce a totalizing effect on the lives of elderly care recipients. Unfortunately, this potential remains largely unrecognized and unregulated at the levels of policy planning and service delivery. It is evident that this lack of awareness derives from the temporal encompassment inherent in the cultural construction of old age. Since the older individual is presumed to have no social future, attention is focused exclusively on the fulfillment of *immediate* needs. Little thought is given to the long-term effects of structured living situations on the changing self-concept and psycho-social development of the older person.

One must consider that the majority of older people who are forced to fall back upon the protection of the state have first exhausted all available means for maintaining independence within the community. Already suffering from lowered self-esteem and a feeling of impotence, they regard their acquiescence to a social worker as the final abdication of rights and responsibility. They are easily intimidated and highly vulnerable to manipulation by those in authority. For example, the owner of the boarding home where Matthew Parsons lived had no legal precedent for confining her charges to the premises. It was just "more convenient" for her to do so. Yet all of them abided by her orders; the reality of their situation offered little opportunity for protest. Any attempt to reassert control over one's surroundings (as in the case of Matthew Parsons) was considered a symptom of deviance.[6]

Foster care constituted a significant improvement for Matthew because the relationship between "supplicant" and "provider" was mediated by the establishment of fictive kin ties. He was placed with a large family who had already accepted two other elderly men as foster care recipients. One of these men, called "Grandpa" by the family, was too frail to do any work. The other was responsible for collecting firewood, feeding the family dog, and doing odd jobs around the house. Matthew served as confidant and companion for the children and was

6. Several years after Matthew left this boarding home, the owner was stabbed by another resident.

sometimes expected to help the head of household, a minister, with church activities.

The establishment of kin ties contributed to the rapid improvement of Matthew's self-concept for several reasons. First, it suggested that the family had fully understood and willingly accepted the responsibility for his care. Second, the substitution of kin status served to shift this responsibility from a context of institutional charity to one of mutual recognition. In contrast to Matthew's former status as an indigent stranger, he was now entitled to the privileges accorded a contributing member of the social unit. Finally, the fictive kin status gave Matthew the freedom to express his needs openly, without guilt about seeming ungrateful or fear of rejection and abandonment. Once these conditions had been met, this "suicidal" old man resumed his place as a productive member of the artistic community.

For the most part, however, protective care programs for the dependent elderly have come to be regarded as terminal environments or, at best, as transitional way stations on the road to a nursing home. It is not surprising to discover that some social workers cannot see beyond the maintenance of "good working relationships" between themselves and the operators of protective care establishments. The policy structure within which the social worker operates does not provide avenues or incentives for ensuring continued outward mobility among those older individuals who desire to remain socially active. This desire will continue to be thwarted until the older person's ongoing "engagement" with the world comes to be recognized and respected by those charged with creating alternative life environments for older people.

[5]

Neighborly Senior Services

The gift, to be true, must be the flowing of the giver unto
me, correspondent to my flowing unto him.

> Ralph Waldo Emerson
> *Essays, Second Series*

The little house on the fringes of downtown St. Petersburg looked abandoned. The grass out front was knee-high;
the screens were torn where thieves had broken in repeatedly.
This was the house where Sarah Myerson had lived for twenty
years. She was ninety, overweight, and partially deaf. For exercise she did all the laundry by hand and walked through each
room five times every day. She never, ever went outside.

Paul Byron, age unknown, lost his vocal cords and part of his
throat to cancer. Social workers had tried to "help" him, but he
wasn't having any of that. Paul liked to keep moving, so he
stored his few belongings in an old, beat-up car. Each night, he
found a quiet place to park and went to sleep.

Will Schulz and his wife, Lana, never learned to speak much
English. It wasn't easy to make friends, but they had each
other. Then Lana developed Alzheimer's disease. Most of the
time she occupied herself with polishing imaginary furniture.
Will never knew, though, when she might take a notion to go
for a walk and not come back. She rarely slept; he was afraid to
sleep.

There are many people like Sarah, Paul, and the Schulzes in

St. Petersburg. For a variety of reasons, they have gradually become alienated from their surroundings and isolated from kin and peer support networks. Much of the research that has gone into the writing of this book represents my attempt to understand how and why such estrangements occur. The reasons are not always obvious, nor are they always related to a history of poverty or dependence.

Sarah, for instance, moved to St. Petersburg from New York at age seventy to share her brother's home. Neither had ever married. The brother eventually died, leaving Sarah alone but not really lonely. A retired professional with several advanced degrees and a modest pension, she was comfortable with her books and the company of a few good friends and neighbors.

Gradually, inflation ate away at Sarah's pension; the house needed repairs she couldn't afford. She began to have trouble walking and hearing. Old friends died, moved away, or just stopped coming around. For a woman who had enjoyed a long life of independence, the situation had its ironic element:

"When I was seventy, I realized that I was probably going to live a lot longer," Sarah explained. "So I made myself a plan—seventy to ninety. Now I've reached ninety, and I don't have another plan!"

I have brought to this work the conviction that alienation in old age is constructed, not natural, and that it can be reversed through enlightened social planning and policy. Sarah, Paul, and the Schulzes shared one modest but clearly defined expectation, to remain independent no matter what the physical and emotional cost might be. Within the traditional structure of services, their options were nonexistent. Yet all three received help through an independent social agency that has made the best use—in fact and in spirit—of the opportunities provided by the Older Americans Act of 1965.

Neighborly Senior Services (NSS), formerly called "The Neighborly Center," developed in the mid-1960s from a Na-

tional Council on the Aging project known as FIND (Friend-
less, Isolated, Needy, Disabled). Project FIND staff were
among the first to establish meals-on-wheels programs, and the
first to open an adult day care center in the United States. The
original program served about 25 people in day care and provided meals for an additional 150.

In 1984, NSS is providing four thousand five hundred meals
daily through a variety of adult day care, congregate dining,
and meals-on-wheels programs. It will reach out to more than
eight hundred homebound elderly like Sarah Myerson with
one-on-one case management programs. It will provide services for the deaf, education through cable television, respite
care for the families of dependent elderly, day care specifically
for Alzheimer's patients, senior center facilities, seminars on
successful aging, and a variety of other needed services. It will
do all of this with three hundred staff members, five thousand
volunteers, and very limited financial support from the city of
St. Petersburg.

The bulk of Neighborly Senior Services' nine million dollar
yearly budget comes from federal and state sources through
the Older Americans Act.[1] In 1982, the organization asked
St. Petersburg for $251,000 in matching funds; they received
$20,000. In 1983 they requested $62,000, based on a conserva-
tive "fair share" estimate of city residents served. They were
granted $17,300.[2]

It's not surprising that a city so dedicated to changing its image would hesitate to spend money on services for the frail and
dependent elderly. Yet in the downtown area, where the median age is seventy-three, the old will become older, sicker,
and poorer before they fade away. With increasing private support, NSS continues to serve as a model for the formation of social policy based on common sense, cost-effectiveness, and a

1. This has included, at various times, Titles III, IV, VII, and XX.
2. In 1983, contributions from all local governments in Pinellas County totaled
$95,893.

deep regard for the humanity of the older person. Detailed discussion of the two programs with which I am most familiar is presented below.

Adult Day Care

"Adult day care" is an unfortunate choice of words; it implies that the elderly are to be treated like children in accord with the most debasing stereotypes about old age. Thus I was prepared for the worst when I first learned that there was adult day care in St. Petersburg. What I discovered was the most vital, future-oriented, and supportive constellation of services currently available to older people in Pinellas County.

On my first visit to an NSS adult day care site I was handed a small brochure that stated the goals and philosophy of the program. Excerpts from that brochure convinced me that this was a place worth visiting again, and again:

> The Adult Day Care Program provides a pleasant, protective environment for persons sixty years of age and older who should not remain in their own homes alone but do not require institutional care.
>
> This program allows working families and those with other responsibilities the comfort of knowing that their elderly relatives are being properly cared for during the day. The participants are able to remain as a part of the family unit, secure in the knowledge that they are still wanted.
>
> With the goal of delaying and/or preventing institutionalization, this program assists the individual in maintaining his independence.
>
> At the day care centers, under the supervision of a trained staff, elderly participants have the opportunity to make friends, to participate in various activities, to be regarded as individuals, and to come to the realization that they are still a part of the society in which they live.

It is significant that the organizers of this program chose the term "participant" over the customary "recipient" or "client." The word participant suggests active, reciprocal engagement as opposed to passive dependency and social impotence. The individual who "participates" in a program is entitled to reap the benefits of membership. By structuring the initial enrollment of older people in this way, the adult centers are able to circumvent many of the demeaning implications attached to the concept of social services for the dependent elderly.

The six adult day care sites maintained by Neighborly Senior Services vary in character according to their location. The particular site where I spent one day per week for over a year was housed in a small building owned by a local church. The floors were worn, the furniture was mismatched, and the fifty-five participants had to walk carefully to avoid tripping over each other. There were few complaints, however.

Participants were picked up at their homes by minibus in the morning and returned in mid-afternoon. Each person determined his or her own schedule; some chose to come Monday through Friday while others limited their attendance to once or twice per week. Each participant was escorted from the bus individually and greeted with an offer of coffee and donuts. Since participants who had problems at home were usually still fuming when they got off the bus, staff members often utilized this time to pinpoint issues that might require intervention. If a participant seemed unusually hungry, for instance, a staff member might inquire what he or she had eaten for breakfast. Occasionally it was discovered that a participant who seemed argumentative or grouchy had just been threatened with eviction or placement in a nursing home.

Throughout the day, the center offered a low-key, low-budget schedule of recreational, educational, and entertainment programs. Each person was encouraged to participate in accord with his or her known interests; attendance at lunch was the only "mandatory" activity. Some people were joiners, ready for any lecture, movie, sing-along, or exercise program that came their way. Others preferred to socialize with friends or merely to sit and observe.

The average nursing home activity director would probably be appalled at the seemingly haphazard manner in which adult day care activities were organized. Neighborly Senior Services participants liked it just fine. In fact, their option to select their activities—or no activities—distinguished this program from many other social services for older people. Often, the well-meaning but misguided workers who staff such places will pressure the elderly to participate in crafts and games that they find uninteresting or inappropriate. (Anyone who has been to a nursing home Halloween party will know the ramifications of this.) Easily intimidated and afraid to say no, the older person is made to feel like a kindergarten child who must be "kept busy" at all times.

Helping the older person to remain within the family was a clearly stated goal of NSS adult day care. Will Schulz, mentioned earlier in this chapter, was unwilling to place his wife in a nursing home and unable to care for her alone. Their lives might have ended tragically had it not been for the adult center, which provided Lana with a safe place to go while Will did his errands and got some sleep. As it was, Lana was able to remain at home until her death.

Jim Till, another day care participant, lived with his children and grandchildren. Confined to a wheelchair, he was obliged to stay home alone during the day while the rest of the family were at work or school. The adult center gave this gregarious, alert man a new social environment and a new set of friends.

Less than half of the participants at this particular adult day care center lived with relatives, however. Many lived alone or, like Matthew Parsons, in congregate housing situations. These people found the secondary services offered by the center invaluable in their efforts to maintain independence. The center provided a weekly bus trip to a neighborhood supermarket, for

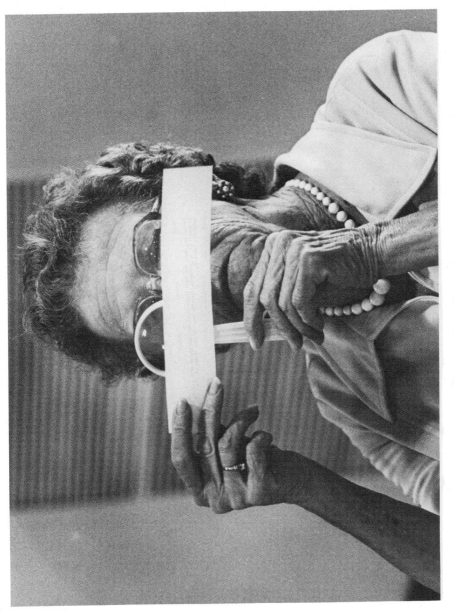

16. Checkers game, Neighborly Senior Services

17. Exercise class, Neighborly Senior Services

[125]

18. Neighborly Senior Services

instance. A staff member or volunteer went along to help carry bundles and to fill orders from those participants who found the excursion too strenuous. Participants who utilized the shopping opportunity regularly did so because they had no other access to the variety and lower prices available in large grocery stores.

The center also offered a weekly banking trip, complete with tactful advice for people who had difficulty managing checkbooks or keeping accurate account of their bills. There was individual transportation to doctors' appointments and appointments at other social services agencies. When participants returned from these appointments with prescriptions or "paperwork" in hand, there was always someone ready to help puzzle out the details.

One day a woman returned from her doctor's office with two new prescriptions. As usual, a staff member asked if she understood what each one was for and how the medicine was to be taken. She shook her head, then held out the two bottles, which bore complicated directions in very small print. "I can't read it," she said with some embarrassment. Assuming that the print was too small for her to see, the center director colorcoded the bottles and then wrote out the directions for each on a large scrap of paper. The woman looked hopeful for a moment, then lowered her eyes. It wasn't her vision, she explained; she just didn't know how to read.

Problems like this can leave the older person embarrassed, confused, and occasionally endangered. Vigilant as they were, the day care center staff were unable to avert one near-tragedy involving an older woman and her medications. A regular participant at the center, this woman began showing signs of mental confusion. Eventually she was taken to a hospital, where it was discovered that she was suffering from adverse drug interactions. A day care center volunteer offered to go to the woman's apartment and collect all her medications so that the problem could be straightened out. The volunteer found an old shoe box filled with pills and capsules, none of them bottled. Unable to remember which was which, the sick woman had fallen into the habit of simply reaching into the box and taking a few pills at random whenever she wasn't feeling well.

Such stories were distressingly common, and were not limited to the relationship between doctor and patient. Needed services were so surrounded by red tape and sheer legwork that they remained virtually out of reach for many of the frail elderly. For them, the day care center became a personal advocate, a sort of substitute irate uncle with political connections.

Even so, the wheels of justice moved slowly. Adult day care participants were never pressured to share their problems, and many struggled mightily on their own before asking for help. One man made several trips to the Social Security office in an attempt to get his payment schedule activated. His employment records were more or less in order, but his birth had never been recorded. Unable to prove his age, he was denied payment for almost two years. The matter was cleared up when the adult center learned of his problem and vouched for the fact that he was indeed sixty-five years old.

Overall, the adult day care program sought to isolate the most serious obstacles faced by those frail elderly who desired to remain functioning members of the community. Attention was focused on negotiating each problem as it arose, without disturbing the hard-earned social equilibrium already established by each participant. While considering itself a "protective" environment, the organization's approach remained qualitatively different from the wholesale restructuring of lives practiced by the state, and often by the families of older people as well.

The adult day care center had no financial criteria for enrollment; older people from all backgrounds and all walks of life found its services vital to their continued independence and ongoing personal development. Possibilities for growth and accomplishment, no matter how small, were always nurtured. In the words of one participant, a long-term psychiatric patient who had returned to the world after half a lifetime in a dependent, timeless setting: "I feel good, and I feel happy. Mama wanted to know why did I like to come out here. I told her 'cause I felt like I'm *needed* out here, and I *enjoy* out here. Everybody's nice to me. . . . They don't 'buke you around, *boss* you around, so you just happy here. I stay so long here an then I want to go home. But she laughed at me this morning, she say, 'You know when the bus comin, don't you?' I say, 'Yes'm, seems like I knows the days now. The days comin to me more.'"

Nutrition Programs

Neighborly Senior Services provides an average of four thousand five hundred hot meals daily through its congregate dining and meals-on-wheels programs. For many of those who receive meals-on-wheels, the daily visit from a meal delivery volunteer provides a primary source of contact with the social community. Congregate dining is an intermediate concept, aimed at the older person who is physically mobile but still unlikely to maintain a nutritionally balanced diet. A total of twenty-eight congregate dining sites are scattered throughout the county in easily accessible facilities such as churches and recreation halls.

The significance of the congregate dining concept for St. Petersburg's downtown retirees cannot be appreciated without awareness of the need fulfilled by this program. My own observations of activity around the numerous small restaurants and cafeterias of the downtown section have shown me that taking at least one meal a day away from home can often become a life necessity for the older person who lives alone. Many widowed men simply do not know how to cook, and their frequent dependence on a haphazard combination of snack foods and alcohol can lead to malnutrition. Widowed females face another set of problems. They often report that preparing food and eating alone is the single most depressing aspect of their daily routine. One informant told me:

"My husband and I never had any children. We both worked during the day, so we really looked forward to relaxing together in the evenings. Dinner time was a ritual of togetherness. I always set the table with good china and tried to make everything look nice.

"After he died, I found that I had no appetite at all. Coming home and eating alone was the worst part of the day; it reminded me too much of what I had lost. When I realized that I was beginning to neglect myself, I set the table again the way we used to do. Even now, I use the best dishes every night. It's become something special that I do just for myself these days, but it makes dinner time worthwhile."

A social worker in her early sixties, this woman realized fully that the death of a spouse can bring about a drastic reduction in one's self-esteem. The routines of work and home life provide points of orientation against which the individual can periodically take measure of his or her self-worth. This is particularly crucial when a couple sell their home and leave relatives and friends to move to Florida. Eventually one dies, and the survivor wakes up alone in a strange city, surrounded by people who do not really "know" him or her. With all familiar points of orientation gone, the person must inevitably ask how much is worth doing for oneself. This is a difficult question, and one that is rarely confronted until we find ourselves truly alone.

Thus, aside from the fact that many older people do not have the energy and/or skills to shop for and prepare their own meals, eating in restaurants often becomes a necessary psychological indulgence. In a small but significant way, dining out provides the opportunity to be recognized, waited on, to see and be seen by other people. The congregate dining concept expands upon these needs and extends the privilege to those who cannot afford the luxury of dining out regularly. Participants register for meal schedules on a weekly basis. They receive nutritionally balanced hot meals, paid for through contributions according to their means. The atmosphere is friendly and informal; participants are offered every opportunity to socialize and to create new friendships. The congregate dining program provides a dignified, constructive approach to fulfilling both the immediate physical and extended social needs of people who would otherwise dine alone, or not at all.

Throughout this book I have stressed the need to develop an awareness of how unspoken cultural assumptions shape our perceptions of the elderly and how these perceptions influence, in very real ways, the older person's self-concept. It is not enough to recognize that the low-income or disabled elderly are often unable to secure the basic necessities of life. Social service programs based on the mere recognition of existing conditions can never approach a true satisfaction of these people's needs. Indeed, surface problems are often alleviated at the expense of far more valuable things such as personal autonomy and the right to maintain dignity and self-respect. That this should be so is a sad commentary on our ability to communicate with the aged, or to consider our own inevitable destiny without hestitation, self-loathing, and fear. Neighborly Senior Services has gone further than any organization I know of in its efforts to transcend the cultural construction of old age and to embrace the total physical and social context within which the aging individual has chosen to live.

[6]

Mental Health Care

I sometimes think that I feel things *more* intensely than I
used to, not less. But I am so afraid of appearing ridiculous.
People expect serenity of the old. That is the stereotype,
the mask we are expected to put on. But how many old people *are* serene? . . .

My anger, because I am old, is considered a sign of madness or senility. Is this not cruel? Are we to be deprived
even of righteous anger? Is even irritability to be treated as
a "symptom"?

May Sarton
As We Are Now

For a man his age, Fred Martinson was blessed with unusually good health. He had money in the bank, an avid interest in
gardening, and many friends in the near southside trailer park
where he had lived for a number of years. Fred was a cautious,
methodical man, not prone to bouts of heavy drinking or other
excessive behavior. Neighbors described him as helpful and
friendly. Relatives in his native England looked forward to his
regular visits.

Then Fred underwent a dramatic personality change. It happened right after a visit to the ophthalmologist, when he was
told he would need cataract surgery. Two months later he shut
himself up in his trailer and attempted to cut his throat with a
dull, rusty knife. After two days he was discovered by a neighbor, but not before he had inflicted numerous wounds on his

neck and arms in a futile attempt to find a vital artery. After five days in a local hospital, Fred was referred to a private psychiatrist and sent home. Six days later he was found dead in a shallow creek behind the trailer park, a cement block attached to his belt with a thin length of rope.

"We wonder why," said his neighbor and contemporary, Bill Brower. "The man had everything; he had no financial troubles. But he was determined to do it. That's all I know. . . . You people are making a study of why it happened. I understand that, and I appreciate it, because there's so many on the verge."

The suicide rate for white females ages 80–84 is estimated to be 7.2 per 100,000. Nonwhite males of the same age cohort end their own lives at a rate of 22.9 per 100,000. Yet for white males ages 80–84, the figure is a striking 51.4 (Pfeiffer 1977:655). As a white male age eighty-two, Fred Martinson was at highest risk for suicide.

According to local statistics provided by the St. Petersburg Medical Examiner's office, there were 110 verified suicides in the city during the first seven months of 1980. At least seventy-nine of these involved persons over sixty-four. (Of course, this figure must be considered in light of the fact that about 40 percent of those residing in the survey area were sixty-five or older.) Four cases involved victims over eighty years of age. One man died of self-inflicted gunshot wounds. A second succumbed to an overdose of drugs. An elderly woman asphyxiated herself. The fourth suicide was Fred Martinson.

Suicide attempts among younger people are often interpreted as last-ditch attempts at communication. If reached in time, the young can often be dissuaded from suicide and convinced that a less dramatic statement will bring about desired changes. The elderly are different. "When an old person attempts suicide," writes Eric Pfeiffer, "he almost always fully intends to die" (1977:655). Described by a close friend as "dedicated to getting out of this world," Fred was one of those who succeeded.

This difference is owing at least in part to the different problems faced by young and old. Transitional crises such as marital or family discord, failure at work or school, and short-term financial difficulties are a few of the problems most commonly associated with suicide attempts. Fred Martinson, who had worked as an elevator operator, was long retired and had sufficient savings to cover most emergencies. He had been widowed for fifteen years. He seemed, outwardly at least, to have weathered most of the short-term stresses associated with retirement and the loss of his wife.

Among older people, suicide is often linked to long-term, cumulative situations and chronic depression. Yet Fred's precipitating crisis *appeared* to be transitional—fear of an impending operation. Friends counseled him repeatedly, assuring him that cataract surgery was safe, the prognosis was excellent, and his stay in the hospital would be brief. What was he really afraid of?

"He was nice to everybody, congenial to everybody, but you never know," one neighbor remarked as he pointed to his heart, "what's inside. Fred was kind of a deep subject."

Martinson's close friend, Bill Brower, was equally baffled as he tried to retrace the events that led to the suicide attempts. Hours and days spent listening to Fred had yielded no clear-cut motive. Did he express any long-range anxieties beyond the immediate, irrational fear of blindness?

"He was seeing the psychiatrist up there," Brower offered. "The man told him, definitely, 'If you try it again, they're going to put you in the nuthouse.' I don't think that helped him."

Martinson was referred for psychiatric out-patient care by personnel at the hospital where he was taken by police for emergency treatment. During his first and apparently his *only* visit, the psychiatrist gave him a prescription for Sinequan

[135]

(doxepin HCI), an antidepressant. The unfilled prescription slip was found in his trailer after his death along with a note from the doctor which read: "One capsule each night at bedtime to help sleep and prevent feeling blue." While Martinson rejected the medication, he did tack the note to his bedroom wall in a prominent place.

It is obvious that no psychiatrist would threaten a man like Fred with confinement to "the nuthouse," as Bill Brower vividly put it. But whatever was said, that is the sum total of what Fred *heard*. He related the statement to his friends, mostly elderly men like himself, who also accepted it at face value.

Fred was offered a variety of community-based services after the initial suicide attempt, including adult day care and meals-on-wheels. He rejected them all. Even in the neighborhood bar, with plenty of support from a network of trusted friends, he was incapable of expressing his true feelings.

Aspects of this case remain troubling. It may be that Fred Martinson was chronically depressed, or that he was simply a stubborn old man, tired of living and determined to "get out of this world." Yet the high suicide risk associated with Martinson's age, sex, and social background points to the existence of underlying cultural barriers to suicide intervention. As anthropologist and clinical psychotherapist Ann Parsons wrote with regard to the relationship between patient and clinician: "All other things being equal, the psychotherapist more readily accepts for treatment the office patient who announces himself by saying 'I have been feeling anxious and depressed lately; perhaps it has something to do with my submissiveness toward my wife' than the one who says 'I gotta nerves, my stomach she hurt alla time,' or 'I'm not crazy; maybe my wife is because she called the police and had me locked up'" (Parsons 1969:296). Parsons observed that therapists were less likely to credit patients in the second category with the capacity to develop insight into their own problems. At the same time, the social experiences and cultural values of low-income and immigrant patients often worked against acceptance of the therapeutic setting. Similar barriers may be encountered in the attempt to provide therapeutic intervention for the very old.

Until recently, many psychiatrists remained silent with regard to the mental health concerns of the elderly. According to Robert Butler, "less than two percent of psychiatric time was spent with elderly patients, or less than one hour per week" in the early 1960s (1975:233). Since then, interest in the psychotherapeutic aspects of aging has expanded considerably.[1] Yet while professionals may be responding, albeit slowly, to the psychiatric needs of the aged, many older people themselves continue to refuse mental health care. Others, like Fred Martinson, may be led to therapy, only to reject it before they can really be helped. Among the very old, cultural barriers to acknowledgment of the need for psychiatric intervention must be removed carefully, for they are often anchored deeply in life experience.

Most Americans under the age of sixty-five are familiar with the concept of "mental health." Dime stores are stocked with a variety of self-help manuals. Popular magazines aimed at the young and middle-aged market stress mental health concerns. The traditional high school guidance counselor has been replaced by a team of specialists trained to recognize problems associated with drug use, low self-esteem, and the traumas associated with divorce and relocation. School counseling has reached down to the elementary level as well, offering therapy for troubled eight-and-nine-year-olds (and their parents). Social agencies and religious organizations utilize television and radio to advertise help for depression, child abuse, alcoholism, and marital discord.

The function of community mental health centers is often poorly understood by those from rural backgrounds or those

1. For an overview of behavioral and biological theories of the psychology of aging see *Handbook of the Psychology of Aging*, ed. James E. Birren and K. Warner Schaie (1977).

with little formal education, however (Chu and Trotter 1974). *The elderly often fall into both categories.* Less than ten years ago, 63 percent of those 65 and older did not hold a high school diploma, as compared to 26 percent of the general population ages 18–64. A person in his or her nineties today who has completed secondary school is a member of a slim 18 percent minority.

Fred Martinson was already two years old when Sigmund Freud published *The Interpretation of Dreams*. When the International Psychiatric Association was founded, he was twelve. Psychological studies dealing primarily with the needs of older people did not really appear in any significant numbers until after World War II, when Martinson was already in his fifties.

Thus a true cultural gap emerges when youthful profession-als confront the elderly, low-income client in need of mental health services. Many older people have been taught from childhood to deny or repress "bad thoughts." Some regard anger and dissatisfaction as sinful, punishable emotions. Equipped with little or no understanding of the psychiatrist's role, they tend to regard the need for therapy as a judgment of social failure, punishable by institutionalization. Since suicide is classed as an antisocial, sinful act, the elderly suicidal person is faced with a double fear and a double stigma.[2]

In addition, most St. Petersburg retirees seem to know at least one friend or neighbor who has been declared mentally incompetent and placed under guardianship. The relocated re-tiree cannot count on the traditional system whereby friends

2. Chu and Trotter discuss the failure of federally supported community men-tal health centers to compensate adequately for existing cultural barriers to treat-ment: "Because the centers' program as a whole embodies a fundamentally mid-dle-class model, individual centers are often irrelevant to the poor and minority groups. Traditional programs, planned and operated by middle-class profession-als, are of dubious appropriateness to poverty-area residents who may not con-ceive of their problems as 'emotional' or 'mental' as defined by professionals, and whose experience has taught them to mistrust the existing 'helping' institutions of the dominant white society" (1974:91).

and relatives take over quietly if a person becomes incapable of managing his or her own affairs. Indeed, Florida retirees hear continually of "senile" peers who have been found alone without food or utilities or who have been bilked of their life's savings by con artists. In one legendary local case, for instance, a woman in her late eighties was sold several hundred dollars worth of pregnancy insurance.

The state of Florida has responded with an elaborate system for determining mental competency, a system that involves both psychiatrists and judges. This system itself has become a focus of anxiety, particularly for the older person who has already absorbed the message that senility is an inevitable concomitant of aging.

Fred Martinson's peers were raised to believe that expression of emotion is a sign of weakness; there was sadness but no disapproval in their description of him as a "deep subject." "Real men" channeled anxiety into work or fulfilling hobbies; Fred's garden was the pride of the trailer park. As an elderly widower, Martinson faced additional problems. While the elderly widow must confront a tragic loss, she does not always experience an abrupt change in life routine. The elderly widower, already severed from identification with his job, must assume an entirely new set of roles upon the death of a spouse. Fully "independent" while cared for by his wife, he may find himself ill-equipped, over time, to maintain the burdens of housework, cooking, and laundry.

Even in the absence of debilitating disease, Fred was faced with a slow erosion of independence. He painted a fantasy picture in letters to his relatives in England—a clean, spacious home and a carefree life-style. The reality was something different. While his small garden and walkway were meticulously maintained, the interior of his trailer was hot, cramped, and dirty. The kitchen area was rarely used; the few canned staples on his shelves were covered with dust. The refrigerator was almost empty.

[139]

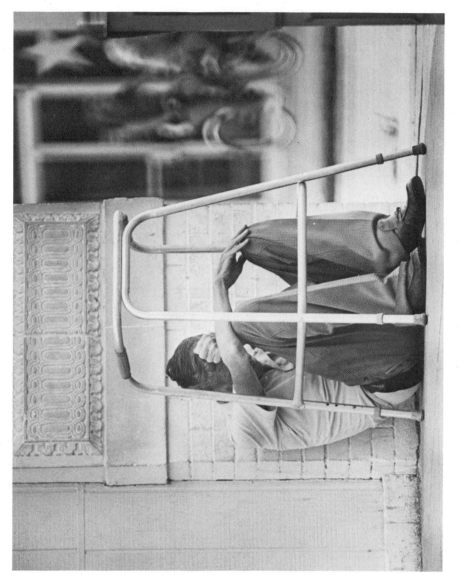

19. Central Avenue at Ninth Street

Following his initial suicide attempt, Fred was urged to enter a boarding home or congregate living facility. He was offered free homemaker services. He rejected all these options. A bad cook and a worse housekeeper, Fred preferred his marginal life-style to the prospect of dependency. That Fred feared some form of institutionalization was further supported by Angelo, a close friend and neighbor. "He didn't want to go into some *home* and be led around," Angelo stressed. "He wasn't a lazy person."

When Fred Martinson's neighbors found him drowned with a weight around his waist, they could have had little doubt that he had committed suicide. Yet for many others, the cause of death is not so obvious. One local authority estimates that for every suicide reported, another older person commits "passive suicide."[3] This description of a woman's home, taken from a newspaper article I wrote about one social intervention program, includes several danger signals of the typical passive suicide:

> The interior of the house is cool, almost cavelike. Or tomblike. The curtains are drawn, the windows closed. . . . The gas in Mrs. Kenney's kitchen has been disconnected for a long time. The stove top now serves as a storage place for unused dishes. There is no refrigerator.[4]

Passive suicides are rarely recognized as such; they are attributed to natural causes, disease, or occasionally to accidents. The victim may slip away quietly, apparently from alcoholism, an untreated heart condition or cancer, even simple starvation. Passive suicides occur gradually and painfully. Without the entry into an intervention network provided by more dramatic suicide attempts, the passive suicide victim is often overlooked entirely.

3. William Simpson, director, Family Service Centers (personal communication).
4. *St. Petersburg Times*, May 4, 1981.

Much has been written about the changing status of the extended family, which has traditionally served as a primary resource for older people. While many of the elderly retain family ties more or less intact, those who migrate to places like St. Petersburg present a special case. Professionals who seek to intervene in the lives of distressed older people are hampered by the absence of a well-established social network. To their clients, they are simply more strangers in an already shifting environment. They cannot always turn to the clients' siblings or children as mediators in their attempts to establish trust and rapport.

Churches have traditionally provided a low-key, non-threatening setting for the older person to get involved in a mental health service network. "Yet over half of the older people [in St. Petersburg] do not go to church," observed St. Petersburg psychiatrist Theodore Machler in 1980. "They [may] have no easy access, there may be no activities [specifically] for them, or they may feel that they can't make a significant contribution."[5] In a 1982 survey I conducted for the *St. Petersburg Times*, only fifteen of the county's estimated five hundred churches and synagogues responded to a newspaper questionnaire on church-sponsored activities for the elderly.[6] More detailed investigation revealed that several ministers and church volunteer co-ordinators who believed they *were* serving the needs of older people offered nothing more than "Bible study" classes and an occasional holiday dinner.

Among the elderly, the decision to commit suicide often comes as the culmination of a long period of social estrangement. Some patients, of course, have long-term patterns of depressive behavior, and these can best be helped through traditional psychotherapy. In other cases, depression can be traced

5. Personal communication. This comment referred primarily to relocated, white retirees.
6. *St. Petersburg Times*, Nov. 20, 1982.

to organic conditions or the interaction of medications. Yet a significant number of suicidal older people cannot be reached through current models for diagnosis and treatment. In these cases, depression is often linked to life situations that can be modified or changed.

Mental health professionals, particularly psychiatrists, rarely encounter low-income elderly clients outside the clinical setting, however. In community mental health centers, where psychiatrists are hired by the hour on a part-time basis, the elderly are often paraded through for office consultations that rarely last more than fifteen minutes. In legal adjudications of competency, where psychiatric opinions are weighed heavily, consulting psychiatrists may see the "defendant" only once, and under conditions of extreme stress.

One local competency case involved a seventy-nine-year-old widow and her son. The woman, who lived alone in a condominium, was invited to visit the son in another state. When she got there she was taken to a nursing home, where her son had made arrangements to have her admitted. After the initial shock wore off, the woman contacted friends in Florida, who had her flown back home. She then sank into a deep depression, attempted suicide, and was temporarily committed to a psychiatric hospital.

The son took this occasion to file competency proceedings against his mother, seeking guardianship of her person and her property. Two court-appointed psychiatrists agreed that the woman was seriously disturbed and recommended that she be declared incompetent.

At this point, a sympathetic nurse became involved on behalf of the hapless widow. She contacted the woman's longtime friends, who testified that she had been "nervous but normal" until she was betrayed by her son. Then the nurse called the woman's other son, who was not aware of what had happened. He told her that his brother, a former prisoner of war in Southeast Asia, had been released from the service due to psy-

20. Downtown alley

chiatric problems of his own. Once informed of these extenuating circumstances, the judge ruled that the woman did not require a guardian of person. Two long-time friends agreed to manage her financial affairs, an arrangement that both the woman and the court found quite acceptable.

How much less humiliating this situation would have been had the psychiatrists looked beyond the incoherent, withdrawn woman before them to uncover the context of her emotional breakdown. Unfortunately, the paradigm of traditional psychotherapy does not dispose doctors to view most events in later life as diagnostically significant. From the apex of adult development, old age is viewed as a decline. This is evident in all the areas of traditional psychology that deal with the older person, from clinical personality studies to laboratory testing of auditory or visual perception and memory. One need not search far for the common denominator that has generated such terms as "disengagement," "role loss," and "roleless role" for sociologists and "regression," "living in the past," and "reality disorientation" for psychologists. In both cases, the ongoing nature of the older person's experience in the world is devalued.

The suicidal aged present a therapeutic paradox; those most in need of assistance are often least likely to find it palatable. At the same time, therapists who serve the low-income elderly are rarely exposed to their life situations—situations to which depression often seems the only "normal" response. Eighty years of accumulated values and expectations cannot be rearranged overnight, but with increased understanding and awareness of the social and physical needs of older patients, a compromise can and must be reached.

Conclusion: *Intelligere est pati*

Living in the world, we live with others and for others, ori-
enting our lives to them. In experiencing them as *others*, as
contemporaries and fellow creatures, as predecessors and
successors, by joining with them in common activity and
work, influencing them and being influenced by them in
turn—in doing all these things we *understand* the behavior
of others and assume that they understand ours. In these
acts of establishing or interpreting meanings there is built
up for us in varying degrees of anonymity, in greater or
lesser intimacy of experience, in manifold intersecting per-
spectives, the structural meaning of the social world, which
is as much our world (strictly speaking, my world) as the
world of others.

> Alfred Schutz
> *The Phenomenology of the Social World*

A small crowd was gathered in downtown Williams Park:
shoppers, winos, idling laborers on their lunch break, and a
few itinerant hippies. An old man sat doubled over on a bench.
His face was pale and drawn, his mouth open. A thin stream of
saliva glinted in the sun as it trailed down from his upper lip.
A patrolman crouched close by, gingerly feeding him oxygen
from a portable respirator.

The crowd was composed mostly of younger people. Old
people shuddered and turned away—too close for comfort.
Things stood still for an agonizing few minutes. The cop spoke
routine words of encouragement: "Can you squeeze my hand?"

[147]

but the usual queries that bind spectators together in a crisis situation were absent. No one had to ask what happened—just another old man down.

The ambulance came, followed by a fire department rescue truck. The attendants took their time. Why not? The smile of a private joke faded as they lugged a stretcher across the grass; it was quickly replaced with a mask of frowning urgency. Public behavior in public places. The man was gently lifted and strapped onto taut canvas. He disappeared, filed away in a yellow tin box with flashing lights.

In his discussion of the dialectic of tragedy, Kenneth Burke writes:

> This is the process embodied in tragedy, where the agent's action involves a corresponding passion, and from the sufferance of the passion there arises an understanding of the act, an understanding that transcends the act. The act, in being an assertion, has called forth a counter-assertion in the elements that compose its context. And when the agent is enabled to see in terms of this counter-assertion, he has transcended the state that characterized him at the start. In this final state of tragic vision, intrinsic and extrinsic motivations are merged. That is, although purely circumstantial factors participate in his tragic destiny, these are not felt as exclusively external, or scenic; for they bring about a *representative* kind of accident, the kind of accident that belongs with the agent's particular kind of character. (1969:38–39)

Residents of St. Petersburg bear witness to many "representative accidents" involving elderly people (see Pearce 1974). The most striking feature of these truly "dramatic" events, however, is that they invariably fail to provoke a sense of dialectical tension among members of the "audience." An old man, beset with numerous health problems, decides to pack up his bags and move to Florida—to freedom. Eventually his strength gives out and he quietly collapses on a public bench, an anonymous stranger in a strange land. He has not escaped at all, but merely substituted a new context for the enactment of his ultimate struggle. No one is surprised, no one feels there is something to learn from the situation. At most, his few acquaintances will remark, "If he knew he was sick he should have stayed up North. Then at least his family could visit him in the nursing home."

It is a terrifying commentary on the state of contemporary society that thousands of elderly people should die alone, among strangers, rather than follow to the end the courses they have been carefully charting for a lifetime. By right, the dramatic impact of this tragic and often repeated scene should jolt observers into recognizing what they have done to others —and, ultimately, to themselves. Yet this act of recognition does not occur. The aging individual is seen as a separate and alien being, subject to rules and regulations that do not govern the behavior of the socially engaged adult. The social community does not accept responsibility for the cultural construction of old age. In fact, aging is not often viewed as a cultural process at all. Its observable manifestations—idleness, alienation, and a breakdown in relations with significant others—are regarded as the mere *effects* of old age, not as cues for the final unfolding of human life on a particular cultural stage.

Alfred Schutz speaks compellingly of the need to achieve, through self-conscious philosophical reflection, a critical understanding of the analytic concepts one selects as tools to uncover meaning: "Whoever, then, wishes to analyze the basic concepts of the social sciences must be willing to embark on a laborious philosophical journey, for the meaning-structure of the social world can only be deduced from the most primitive and general characteristics of consciousness" (1967:12). His statements echo those of Bergson, and the elusive "intuition" he sought to achieve (1911:176-79; 1955:35). The social scientist who cannot reflect on the self as "being-in-the-world" can never hope to employ the analytic tools at his or her disposal for more than the most circumscribed of purposes.

[149]

21. Straub Park, off Beach Drive

A lack of self-reflection is quite evident in the general failure of gerontology to generate humanistic models for the study of later life. It is true that old age itself remains as yet outside the realm of experience for most of us who seek to understand the aging process in cultural as well as physical terms. Yet this does not mean that the young and middle-aged must confine their observations to the quantitative realm. Were personal familiarity or "sameness" to be the sole criterion of understanding, the dialectical relationship between self and other which motivates anthropological inquiry would hold no cathexis. We must somehow strike a counterpoise between externality and internality in order to apprehend the "otherness" of those who are old and alone.

The phenomenon of aging introduces a unique obstacle to the appreciation of "otherness." I first became aware of this problem in the course of studying the relationships between residents and staff in two Massachusetts nursing homes (Vesperi 1975, 1983). I observed that, for the most part, older nurses and aides were measurably more distant and hostile toward patients than were younger women in equivalent positions. The casual observer might expect the reverse to be true, as older nurses were closer to their charges in experience and presumably more sensitive to their needs. Yet, in Sartre's terms, old age truly remains as one of the "unrealizables" (Sartre 1966; de Beauvoir 1972). It is possible to identify old age as a category, and eventually to accept the cultural identification of oneself as old. Yet this bears scant resemblance to the physical and emotional experience of individuals; it is not possible to "realize" old age in relation to the ongoing flow of internal time-consciousness.

Within the nursing home setting, younger staff members could regard the patient as they would any other "sick" person. In discussions about patients, they tended to focus on the presence of infirmities and diseases; they found it possible to sympathize with these problems without threat to their own self-concept. Most older nurses, however, depersonalized their interaction with patients; they regarded them as "difficult cases" suffering from an untreatable, terminal disorder—old age. Perhaps they saw in their patients a foreshadowing of their own demise; to regard the patient as emphatically human was to open the door to a painful realm of introspection.

Those who are old are highly sensitive to the implications of social interactions; those who are old, poor, and alone are even more so. Such sensitivity is crucial to their assessment of how they will be perceived and, more important, how they will be dealt with by society. This concern often creates barriers to communication, and older informants may attempt to re-structure interview situations in order to compensate for per-ceived inequalities. Thus the researcher who enters the field armed with questionnaries should not always expect to obtain "objective" answers to such measures of life satisfaction as "Are you lonely?" "Do you hear from your children often?" and "Do you consider yourself healthy or unhealthy?" Candid responses often constitute admissions of failure for people who must struggle daily to compensate for a variety of culturally con-structed shortcomings.

Fortunately, the long-term, informal relationships estab-lished by anthropologists provide ideal opportunities for older informants to articulate concerns about social networks, health, and self-concept in a nonthreatening context. Once such rela-tionships are established, research goals can be accomplished without violating the dignity of elderly informants or causing them to lose face.

The tendency of older people to draw upon examples and ex-perience from the past must be utilized to the fullest extent in the construction of research designs. While some may object that this approach makes data collection a nonstandardized and unwieldy business, the very nature of the research population makes it inevitable, indeed desirable. A full, varied life of

22. Downtown

eighty or ninety years cannot be compressed into a few hours of computer-programmable questions.

Finally, the format within which research data on the elderly appear must allow for the extended presentation of narrative texts. The encounter between researcher and subject is often critical to an understanding of the dialectical struggle between self-concept and age-stereotyping which the older person must confront. More research is needed to fully identify the recurrent rhetorical devices employed by the elderly in their efforts to clarify their position vis-à-vis others. We may discover that many of the conversational patterns and strategies now classed as indicators of "reality disorientation" or "senility" are really no more—and no less—than the aging individual's attempt to make sense of the cultural disorder we have created.

"You can laugh now, 'cause you don't know about it yet," ninety-two-year-old Selena Harper remembers her mother saying. "But someday you'll be where I am." As Selena discovered, the line between laughter and understanding will ultimately be crossed through direct awareness of old age, and what we have made of it.

Afterword to the Cornell Paperbacks Edition

Here is that strange paradox to which all people cultivating the self by way of the addition method are subject: they use addition in order to create a unique, inimitable self, yet because they automatically become propagandists for the added attributes, they are actually doing everything in their power to make as many others as possible similar to themselves; as a result, their uniqueness (so painfully gained) quickly begins to disappear.

Milan Kundera
Immortality

Some two decades after the initial research that led to this book, green benches are back in style in St. Petersburg. They no longer line the sidewalk as they did in mid-century, café seating for afternoon strollers whose goals for the day included casual conversation. With few exceptions, the new green benches are artfully scattered in groups of two, offering brief respite for solitary shoppers or couples on the go. Some boast light green plastic slats in place of the traditional wood, and some aren't really green at all. People still call them green benches, though, and many regard them as historically neutral symbols of civic pride.

In the Snell Arcade Building, a restored retail complex at the center of downtown, Green Bench Flowers exploits the historic legacy to its fullest. Originally completed in 1929, the Snell Arcade features many of the Mediterranean-style touches that colored the architectural statements made by wealthy Floridians of the period. Almost eighty years later, the building still bespeaks the power of money and the people who wield it to shape and impose their vision of a community's lifestyle. The rear display window of Green Bench Flowers, a decidedly upscale shop, is surrounded by beautiful handmade tiles with intricate patterns. Enshrined behind the glass and surrounded by floral arrangements is a modest green bench, symbol of tradition, hospitality, understated good taste.

Green benches were once shunned as the furniture of "God's waiting room," but St. Petersburg has begun to recultivate the green bench image. Hence one might assume that attitudes toward the downtown's older citizens have shifted as well. I would say instead that the elderly themselves have changed, that those who occupy the category "old" today are a different cohort altogether. Gone are the garrulous transplants who patrolled the sidewalks with a we're-in-it-together sense of community formed in the 1930s. Gone also are the thoughtful African American pioneers who settled neighborhoods that have largely disappeared as well.

Many people who read this book asked how it all turned out. Did the elderly or the city "win"? To pose the question is to confuse a culturally constructed category with the individuals it captures in a demographic moment. St. Petersburg's total population increased only 0.7 percent between 1980 and 1990, but the city has continued to grow younger. According to the 1990 census, the median age in St. Petersburg is 38.6, down from 42.2 in 1984 and 48.1 in 1970. The most precipitous declines have occurred in the downtown census tracts covered in my research; in some neighborhoods the median age fell twenty years or more between 1980 and 1990.

To my knowledge, all of the retirees who participated in the original research for this book have since died. Most of them were poor, and most lived in or near downtown. Some were middle-class or blue-collar folk who were poor because, having retired in the 1950s, they had outlived their ability to account for inflation in financial planning. None put this dilemma more succinctly than Sarah Myerson: "When I was seventy, I realized that I was probably going to live a lot longer. So I made myself a plan—seventy to ninety. Now I've reached ninety, and I don't have another plan!" Others were more recently impoverished by catastrophic or chronic illness. The black elderly I interviewed had been subject to institutionalized racism throughout their entire working lives; jobs with pension plans were denied them and they were also sidestepped by the Social Security system. For this group, work began in childhood on farms in Alabama or Georgia and extended well into the eighth or even ninth decade in St. Petersburg's service economy.

Origins of poverty aside, one thing these people had in common was that almost all were housed to their own satisfaction. From the mid-1970s to the early 1980s I visited the downtown aged in single-family bungalows, apartments, hotels, rooming houses, and trailers. With a few notable exceptions, most who were continuing to live independently expressed pleasure in their surroundings, no matter how modest. None owned cars; theirs was a walking culture with its leisurely pace and low-key but vital opportunities for social interaction. These retirees regarded access to downtown shopping and basic services as a key to their continued independence. Their biggest fear was that the familiar stores would disappear, and in the case of the black elderly, that their very neighborhoods would be obliterated. To a large extent, those fears were realized during their lifetimes.

High-rise, low-income apartments for the elderly are still available, and a new store has replaced Webb City as the major source of groceries for residents of John Knox and Graham Park. The eclectic variety of affordable, elder-friendly housing has been greatly reduced, however. Many of the small hotels and apartment buildings have been razed or converted to other uses; some that remain have deteriorated badly.

[157]

The Sunshine Center, St. Petersburg's multipurpose public facility for the elderly, is still a vital hub of activities, advocacy, information, and services. Neighborly Senior Services also continues to serve as a lifeline for the downtown aged. The agency's adult day care center that served downtown is closed, however, and the need for congregate dining services has declined. The focus is shifting to meals-on-wheels and other in-home services as the high-rise dwellers continue to age in place. And while Neighborly Senior Services remains strongly committed to the low-income elderly, it has broadened its mission statement to include other groups as well. Nonprofit corporations such as this one are forced to reach well beyond their original goals as they are increasingly threatened by the generalized withdrawal of public commitment to social welfare and the concomitant push toward privatization.

The census tract bordering the downtown business district on the south, where the median age is 66.8, continues to be swallowed by development. Neighborhoods to the immediate north are undergoing a subtle but relentless gentrification. New condominium construction is under way downtown, but the goal is to attract working professionals and affluent retirees who prefer an urban lifestyle to the beach or a planned community. The units are designed with formal entertaining in mind, and priced accordingly. One up-and-coming complex on the site of an old hotel kept the hotel's name but replaced its sprawling warren of rooms with twenty-seven "luxury townhomes." According to the promotional brochure, the development "captures the tradition, elegance and grandeur of the past," with the addition of gated, electronically controlled access and parking for two cars per household.

In the 1970s and '80s, when "old" was closely associated with old *people,* many of St. Petersburg's pre–World War II buildings were regarded as impediments to progress and some were demolished. Foremost in the old-equals-bad equation was the Vinoy Hotel, a once-imposing structure that sat vacant and crumbling on the city's waterfront because its owner, a flinty businessman in his eighties who delighted in irritating city officials, would neither sell nor restore it. Instead he leased the building to a series of hopeful but naive entrepreneurs, who routinely announced grand plans for its, and hence the city's, revitalization. Each plan was crushed by financing problems and the sheer enormity of the undertaking, until those who would demolish even this landmark began to speak more boldly. Over bitter protests from preservationists, another nearby hotel did become fodder for a filmed-on-location demolition scene. Optimists found solace in the fact that St. Petersburg would appear in a movie—until that shot was cut from the film's final version.

During this era wide latitude was given to the Bay Plaza Companies, an out-of-town development group in partnership with the city and key commercial interests. Bay Plaza set to work on a $200 million grand plan that encompassed, at least in theory, nine city blocks. There were meetings, presentations, receptions, theme designs and colors, and even a scale model. The vision included multiplex cinemas and restaurants, highest-end retail shopping, a festival marketplace atmosphere, and, of course, ample indoor parking. Problem: lots of old buildings in the way. Problem: some owners were unwilling to sell, and the preservationists were literally kicking up sand. Problem: highest-end retail stores were not so eager after all to establish outlets in downtown St. Petersburg, Florida.

Some old buildings were torn down, and an estimated $50 million in private and public money was spent on the plan before the developers decamped in early 1996. St. Petersburg was left with a new above-ground garage in theme colors, several vacant lots, and almost no street life. By attrition or by design, the sauntering, socializing old folks had all but disappeared from downtown. Younger people came to work, and during lunch hour the shops and restaurants were full. By six P.M., however, boys on skateboards and the homeless had the sidewalks largely to themselves. Something had to be done.

Belatedly gripped by the fever to restore and renovate that has proved commercially successful in Miami and, much closer to home, in Tampa's Ybor City, city officials began to concentrate more heavily on smaller-scale development aimed at revitalizing the old downtown. It helped that the Vinoy was up and running again as the Renaissance Vinoy Resort. An international hotelier had modernized and expanded the waterfront flagship without sacrificing a drop of its Roaring Twenties ambiance. The younger couples and business people who favor the Vinoy today can enjoy a "historic" setting disassociated from the many versions of its historical narrative.

Missing, of course, are the men and women who gave voice to that narrative. Driving by the Vinoy now or occasionally stopping in for coffee on the veranda, I recall what such hotels had meant to my informants. For some, they were the fairyland settings for a special night out. For others who could never have entered the dining rooms without a uniform and a tray, they were magnets that drew the young with powerful promises of work and sustained them, if marginally, as they established families and aged in place.

The same "historicizing" process is at work in the 1920s neighborhood where age segregation made it difficult for me to rent an apartment in 1975 and where, with some sense of irony, I bought two adjacent houses in 1993. Boarding homes and garage apartments are still evident in this neighborhood, but gentrification is a powerful force. With a strong push from the city in the form of vigorous code enforcement, low-income renters are being displaced in favor of families with the means and motivation to restore the large dwellings to single-family use. The previous owners of my home, for example, had carved the adjacent single-family house into three apartments. As new owners, my husband and I were told by the city's board of adjustment that the building must be reconverted. When I protested that two of the units were currently occupied by tenants who were eager to stay, I was informed unabashedly at a public hearing that such small apartments "were not suitable for young people."

Indeed, a study conducted a few years earlier had concluded

that much of the available housing stock was not "suitable" for the young. Almost 70 percent of the city's housing was built between 1950 and 1979; the population increased 87 percent between 1950 and 1960 alone. Few lots remain vacant in St. Petersburg's residential neighborhoods, and a significant percentage of the existing homes are one-story bungalows designed for retirees of modest means. The study predicted that future homeowners would probably tear down the current structures and rebuild to suit the needs of growing, materially acquisitive families.

Our own house had apparently been run as a seasonal boarding home by the previous occupants. When I returned after a week away in November of that first year, the neighbors remarked that they had been visited by "a lady from Canada, looking to rent her room" for the winter season. "Er, we told her that the new owners probably weren't going to do that," they added.

Another nearby property was vacant in 1993; homeless men sometimes camped there, gaining access through a window over the back porch. Soon the house was renovated and then purchased by two young attorneys, one of whom is the incoming president of the neighborhood association. He told me recently that our area, prominently identified by the city's ubiquitous boundary markers as the "Old Northeast," is about to be designated as a historic district.

Old is in, but St. Petersburg's new downtown is not a place where the people I describe in this book could easily live. Nor is it a place where the younger generations of long-established African American families can easily disassociate history and symbol. The baseball stadium erected on the site of the former Gas Plant neighborhood has finally attracted a major league team, causing property values to rise and buoying new optimism among downtown developers. The loss of local landmarks still rankles, however, and the promise of new jobs for black citizens in the area has been very slow to materialize. So little remains of the old community that newcomers can take a handy interstate exit to the stadium without ever troubling themselves over what might have been there before. There is nothing to remind them that their highway and their stadium seats were made possible by the obliteration of historic black neighborhoods, once crowded with businesses, homes, and churches. Some people *cannot* forget, which is one reason tensions flair whenever the promise of a better life through urban renewal is trotted out again.

The relation between signifier and signified is always a dynamic one. In the case of St. Petersburg, the shifting ties between an object and what it means in human terms also offers an interesting lesson in political economy. In the 1970s and '80s, St. Petersburg's attitude toward the old and the material culture they had built and sustained was fused in a culturally constructed perception of decline, decay, and loss. Now the surviving artifacts of 1920s opulence have come full circle. As the condo developers put it, the goal once again is to signify "tradition, elegance and grandeur." The symbols of wealth and power set down by Florida entrepreneurs in the first part of the century have been reclaimed, restored, and even reinvented by a new generation of the upwardly mobile. In his 1988 book, *St. Petersburg and the Florida Dream: 1888–1950*, Raymond Arsenault points out that even the downtown benches were originally a symbol of entrepreneurship, cooked up by Noel A. Mitchell, a salesman on the make. "Always one step ahead of the competition, Mitchell inadvertently created a local institution in 1908 when he placed several bright orange benches in front of his real estate office. Printed in bold letters on the back of each bench was: 'Mitchell, the Sand Man. The Honest Real Estate Dealer. The Man with a Conscience. He Never Sleeps' " (1988: 136). The benches proliferated and, as Arsenault notes, a 1916 city ordinance required that they all be painted a uniform color. It was, of course, the color of money.

References

Arsenault, Raymond. 1988. *St. Petersburg and the Florida Dream: 1888–1950.* Norfolk, Va.: Donning.

Bateson, Gregory. 1972. *Steps to an Ecology of Mind.* New York: Ballantine.

Beauvoir, Simone de. 1972. *The Coming of Age.* Trans. Patrick O'Brian. New York: G. P. Putnam's Sons.

Berger, Peter, and Hansfried Kellner. 1970. "Marriage and the Construction of Reality." In *Recent Sociology no. 2,* ed. Hans Peter Dreitzel. New York: Macmillan.

Bergson, Henri. 1911. *Creative Evolution.* Trans. A. Mitchell. New York: Henry Holt.

———. 1955. *An Introduction to Metaphysics.* Trans. T. E. Hume. Indianapolis: Liberal Arts. (Originally published in 1903.)

Birren, James E., and K. Warner Schaie, eds. 1977. *Handbook of the Psychology of Aging.* New York: Van Nostrand Reinhold.

Bothwell, Dick. 1975. *Sunrise 200.* St. Petersburg: Times Publishing Co.

Burke, Kenneth. 1969. *A Grammar of Motives.* Berkeley: University of California Press.

Butler, Robert. 1975. *Why Survive? Being Old in America.* New York: Harper & Row.

Chu, Franklin D., and Sharland Trotter. 1974. *The Madness Establishment.* New York: Grossman.

Cumming, Elaine, and William E. Henry. 1961. *Growing Old: The Process of Disengagement.* New York: Basic Books.

References

Curtin, Sharon. 1972. *Nobody Ever Died of Old Age*. Boston: Little, Brown.

Dunn, Hampton. 1973. *Yesterday's St. Petersburg*. Miami: E. A. Seemann.

Fantus Company. 1977. *Office Development*. Prepared for St. Petersburg Progress. New York: Fantus.

Freud, Sigmund. 1962. *Civilization and Its Discontents*. Trans. James Strachey. New York: W. W. Norton. (Originally published in 1930.)

——. 1967. *The Interpretation of Dreams*. Trans. James Strachey. New York: Basic Books. (Originally published in 1900.)

Fuller, Walter P. 1972. *St. Petersburg and Its People*. St. Petersburg: Great Outdoors.

Grismer, Karl H. 1924. *History of St. Petersburg*. St. Petersburg: Tourist News Publishing.

Havighurst, Robert J., Bernice L. Neugarten, and Sheldon S. Tobin. 1968. "Disengagement and Patterns of Aging." In *Middle Age and Aging*, ed. Bernice Neugarten. Chicago: University of Chicago Press.

Hendricks, C. Davis, and Jon Hendricks. 1976. "Concepts of Time and Temporal Construction among the Aged, with Implications for Research." In *Time, Roles, and Self in Old Age*, ed. Jaber F. Gubrium. New York: Human Sciences.

Hurley, Frank J., Jr. 1977. *Surf, Sand and Post Card Sunsets: A History of Pass a Grille and the Gulf Beaches*. St. Petersburg: Great Outdoors.

Husserl, Edmund. 1964. *The Phenomenology of Internal Time-Consciousness*. Trans. James S. Churchill. Bloomington: Indiana University Press. (Originally published in 1928.)

Jackson, Jacquelyne J. 1980. *Minorities and Aging*. Belmont: Wadsworth.

Keith, Jennie B. 1982. *Old People as People: Social and Cultural Influences on Aging and Old Age*. Boston: Little, Brown.

——. 1983. "Age and Informal Interaction." In *Growing Old in Different Societies*, ed. Jay Sokolovsky. Belmont: Wadsworth.

Liebow, Elliot. 1967. *Tally's Corner: A Study of Negro Street Corner Men*. Boston: Little, Brown.

Maddox, George L. 1964. "Disengagement Theory: A Critical Evaluation." *The Gerontologist* 4:80-83.

—— and James Wiley. 1976. Introduction, *Handbook of Aging and the Social Sciences,* ed. Robert Binstock and Ethel Shanas. New York: Van Nostrand Reinhold.

Maranda, Pierre. 1972. Introduction, *Mythology,* ed. Pierre Maranda. Baltimore: Penguin.

Mead, George Herbert. 1956. *On Social Psychology*. Chicago: University of Chicago Press.

Merleau-Ponty, Maurice. 1962. *Phenomenology of Perception*. Trans. Colin Smith. London: Routledge & Kegan Paul.

——. 1964. "Phenomenology and the Sciences of Man." Trans. James M. Edie. In *The Primacy of Perception,* ed. James M. Edie. Chicago: Northwestern University Press.

Minkowski, Eugene. 1970. *Lived Time: Phenomenological and Psychopathological Studies*. Trans. Nancy Metzel. Evanston: Northwestern University Press. (Originally published in 1933.)

Moynihan, Daniel P. 1965. *The Negro Family: The Case for National Action*. Washington: Government Printing Office.

Myerhoff, Barbara G. 1978. *Number Our Days*. New York: E. P. Dutton.

Oriol, William E. 1982. *Aging in All Nations: A Special Report on the United Nations World Assembly on Aging*. Washington: The National Council on the Aging.

Osterbind, Carter C. 1976. *Older People in Florida: A Statistical Abstract*. Gainesville: Center for Gerontological Studies and Programs, University of Florida Press.

Parsons, Ann. 1969. *Magic, Belief, and Anomie*. New York: Free Press.

Pearce, Don. 1974. *Dying in the Sun*. New York: Charterhouse.

Pfeiffer, Eric. 1977. "Psychopathology and Social Pathology." In *Handbook of the Psychology of Aging,* ed. James E. Birren and K. Warner Schaie. New York: Van Nostrand Reinhold.

References

Register, Jasper C. 1981. "Aging and Race: A Black-White Comparative Analysis." *Gerontologist* 21:4.

St. Petersburg, City of. 1975. *Multi-Service Citizen Survey for the City of St. Petersburg*. Prepared by Management Improvement Department.

Sartre, Jean-Paul. 1963. *Search for a Method*. Trans. Hazel E. Barnes. New York: Alfred Knopf.

———. 1966. *Being and Nothingness*. Trans. Hazel E. Barnes. New York: Washington Square.

———. 1976. *Critique of Dialectical Reason*. Trans. Alan Sheridan-Smith. London: NLB.

Schutz, Alfred. 1967. *The Phenomenology of the Social World*. Trans. George Walsh and Frederick Lehnert. Chicago: Northwestern University Press. (Originally published in 1932.)

———. 1971. *Collected Papers I: The Problem of Social Reality*. The Hague: Martinus Nijhoff. Third edition.

Sokolovsky, Jay, and Carl Cohen. 1981. "Being Old in the Inner City: Support Systems of the SRO Aged." In *Dimensions: Aging, Culture and Health*, ed. Christine L. Fry. Brooklyn: J. F. Bergin.

———. 1983. "Networks as Adaptation: The Cultural Meaning of Being a 'Loner' among the Inner-City Elderly." In *Growing Old in Different Societies*, ed. Jay Sokolovsky. Belmont: Wadsworth.

Terkel, Studs. 1975. *Working*. New York: Avon.

Vesperi, Maria D. 1975. "Symbolic Parameters." Unpublished paper.

———. 1983. "The Reluctant Consumer: Nursing Home Residents in the Post-Bergman Era." In *Growing Old in Different Societies*, ed. Jay Sokolovsky. Belmont: Wadsworth.

Ward, Russell A. 1984. "The Marginality and Salience of Being Old: When Is Age Relevant?" *Gerontologist* 24:3.

Index

[167]

Index

The Anthropology of Contemporary Issues

A SERIES EDITED BY
ROGER SANJEK

About the Author

Maria D. Vesperi, a former editorial writer and columnist for the *St. Petersburg Times,* is Associate Professor of Anthropology at New College and a trustee of the Poynter Institute for Media Studies.

Library of Congress in Publication Data

Vesperi, Maria D.
    City of green benches.

    (Anthropology of contemporary issues)
    Bibliography: p.
    Includes index.
    1. Aged—Florida—Saint Petersburg. 2. Aged—
Services for—Florida—Saint Petersburg. I. Title.
II. Series.
HQ1064.U6F67 1985   305.2'6'0975963   84–27408
ISBN 0–8014–9322–6 (alk. paper)